# Live at the Forbidden City

## Musical Encounters in
## China and Taiwan

### Dennis Rea

Blue Ear Books
www.blueearbooks.com
7511 Greenwood Ave N, Box 400
Seattle, WA 98103

www.dennisrea.com

www.liveattheforbiddencity.com

BLUE EAR BOOKS

Published in 2015 by
Blue Ear Books
7511 Greenwood Ave N, Box 400
Seattle, WA 98103
USA

www.blueearbooks.com
www.fiftyfiftybooks.com

ISBN: 978-0-9844063-4-0

*Credits:*

Cover Design:
  Jason Kopec, tojasonkopec@gmail.com
Book Composition:
  Jennifer Haywood, Blue Ear Books, Seattle, WA
Printer:
  Scott Morris, Morris Printing Services, Arkansas City, KS, www.morrisprint.com

Cover photo: Curtain Call, 1991 Sichuan-China International TV Festival
© Spike Mafford 1991 www.spikemafford.com

# TABLE OF CONTENTS

*Musicians are always the
best ambassadors.*

— Serge Koussevitsky


*If you open the window,
some flies are bound to get in.*

— Deng Xiaoping


*Even a musician can be an
important witness to history.*

— *Seattle Times* writer Bruce Ramsey

# INTRODUCTION

## TO THE BLUE EAR BOOKS EDITION

In June of 2013 I received an inquiry from National Public Radio correspondent Louisa Lim, who wanted to interview me for a book she was writing to commemorate the 25th anniversary of the 1989 Tiananmen Massacre. In the course of her research, Lim had learned that a similar calamity had befallen the inland city of Chengdu at the same time as the events in Beijing, though it had gone largely unreported due to the foreign press's fixation on what was happening in the capital. Digging deeper, she had come across my lengthy account of the concurrent events in Chengdu in *Live at the Forbidden City*—the only detailed description published in English for many years. We discussed the incident at length over the phone, and much of what I described in that conversation and in the pages of *Live at the Forbidden City* later surfaced in Lim's book *The People's Republic of Amnesia: Tiananmen Revisited*, published on June 4, 2014.

My conversation with Lim dredged up a lot of painful, harrowing memories, as I mentally reenacted those scenes of bloody chaos on the streets of Chengdu. It also sent me back to my own published account and gave me a new appreciation for its continuing relevance. Little did I know back in '89 that my narrative, hastily penned while the tragic debacle was still fresh in mind, would stand as one of exceedingly few eyewitness accounts to appear in the decades to follow.

Around the same time, Ethan Casey, an author and humanitarian of international renown whom I'm proud to call a close friend, got in touch to ask if I'd be interested in republishing my book on the new Blue Ear Books imprint that he'd recently launched with fellow author Bill Steigerwald. Ethan felt strongly that, with the 25th anniversary of Tiananmen approaching, *Live at the Forbidden City* deserved a second life with a new, hopefully wider audience than I had reached with the initial self-published edition. While that edition had been very warmly received by a fair number of readers, as a self-published effort it remained largely under the radar of the wider reading public. I gratefully took Ethan up on his generous offer and am honored to share the result.

Apart from adding a new Introduction and Afterword, I've taken the opportunity to chisel away at the prose here and there, tighten up some facts, update the graphic design, and modify a few passages with the benefit of longer historical hindsight. Otherwise, the narrative remains largely as it unfolded in the previous edition. It's my sincere hope that first-time readers will find *Live at the Forbidden City* as informative—and fun—to read as it was to live, and that those who've come back for seconds will appreciate the enhancements to this second edition. *Xiang qian!*

Dennis Rea<br>
Seattle, September 2014

# FOREWORD

## by Stuart Dempster

When Dennis Rea begins *Live at the Forbidden City* with "This isn't your everyday gig," it is as though a catapult has launched me into somewhere incredible, even mysterious. In short order I become enamored with the duality of gutsy stories and self-effacing humor that Dennis has obviously lived and breathed. *Live*, dotted with moving and perceptive documentary photos by Spike Mafford and others, is written from the heart with abandon, compassion, depth, integrity, perseverance, and strength. There are many events and situations totally unpredictable, and nearly as many that almost defy description. Dennis excites me due to his presence, his awareness, and commitment to the moment in writing this book, and his apparent savoring of every experiential morsel during his time abroad.

While this was written in the context of topical events during the late 1980s and early to mid-1990s, China has continued to cascade headlong into arresting, copious change. Dennis was there precisely at a time when there were landmark changes not only in China's sense of itself but also its position in the world economy and political order. Rare it is to have this view on such a watershed moment. Certainly there were few Westerners there in a position to observe let alone write about such a time, but I also wonder how many Chinese were recognizing the significance of what they themselves were living and witnessing. This marvelous little book offers amazing windows into a tremendously important historical moment, and offers an equally amazing window into Dennis Rea himself.

3

Dennis went to China to teach English, but he also made sure to take his guitar. Of the many wacky stories encountered, some of the earliest have to do with—how shall I put it—instrument care and maintenance. It was not long before a few of his language students were cautiously asking him questions about music in the West. With his guitar, and through his multifaceted gifts and talents, he made important contributions to the opening of new musical experiences. These activities offered opportunities to teach not only musical ideas, but also cultivate memorable relationships through cross-cultural sharing of music with the Chinese people he encountered. Along the way Dennis learned much about Chinese music and, in the process of writing about these various experiences, demonstrates with clarity how political changes impact the evolution of music.

It will surprise me greatly if *Live* does not find its way into bibliography listings as China scholars set about sorting out what happened at that time. It is fantastic to have this energetic and spirited book come forth precisely at a time when China is discovering its own sense of itself with regard to this modern era, and the West is discovering the powerhouse that China has become, let alone its future. Citing certain chapter headings hints at the journey ahead: "Stranger in a Strange Band," "Anguish as a Second Language," "The Great Wall of Sound," "Pandasonic," "Ain't Nothing but a Hongbao," "The Gang of Formosa," "The Feelmore East," and "Taiwannabes," to name but a few, provide an incredible tease as to what is in store. Just try and guess the source of some of those titles—are they made up? Are they a reference to something more?

While there are many parallels to my own time in Europe during 1959-60 as a musician in the Seventh Army Symphony,[1] there are also many differences. One similarity is that traveling to Europe in the late '50s was nearly as exotic as going to Asia in the '90s. However, where my experiences tended toward being amusing, goofy, and downright silly, Dennis' compelling experiences, while just as

---

1    Canarina, John, *Uncle Sam's Orchestra: Memories of the Seventh Army Symphony*, 1998: Rochester, NY, University of Rochester Press.

surreal, occasionally border on being at the cliff's edge. Dennis is all too aware of the Chinese military presences that were surrounding him. Considering that in the context of a communist regime with its secret police, it is not surprising that there are stories that document the sometimes bizarre, Byzantine, cumbersome, outrageous, and time-consuming government regulations. Voilá! A near-perfect combination of ingredients emerges.

Of all the styles of music I play, rock has seldom been in my repertoire. Yet I have known Dennis as colleague (Sun Ra retrospective concerts), friend (Seattle Improvised Music Festival contexts), and student (he wrote lovingly in Seattle's *The Tentacle*[2] about my teaching Multi Media Music at University of Washington). I have neither been to, nor had musical encounters in, China or Taiwan—although as a child it was suggested that I could dig straight down through the earth and arrive in China. I find myself both thrilled with *Live at the Forbidden City* and writing a foreword for it. What can I be thinking? I recognize the excellent storytelling, of course, but also my own somewhat parallel experiences. Through the immediacy and intimacy that Dennis imparts in his journey, there comes a moment when I state with absolute delight, "You can't make this stuff up!" Reading *Live*, while I make only a short, albeit fantastic, whirlwind tour of Taiwan, I can say with enthusiasm and amazement that I have been to China at last!

Stuart Dempster
Seattle, January 2007

*Stuart Dempster is a Sound Gatherer, trombonist, composer, didjeriduist, et al., and Professor Emeritus at the University of Washington. He has recorded for numerous labels including Columbia, Nonesuch, and New Albion. A leading figure in development of trombone technique and performance, Dempster published his landmark book* The Modern Trombone: A Definition of Its Idioms *in 1979.*

---

2    Rea, Dennis, "Dempster: A Class Act," *The Tentacle*, April–May 2000.

# Chinese Pronunciation Key

The following simplified key is provided to assist readers in pronouncing Chinese words and names that appear in the text. With the exception of names of people and places in Taiwan, which until recently followed the Wade-Giles system of Romanization, I have opted to use the more widely implemented Pinyin system of Romanization developed in Mainland China. Note that the key below is not intended to be comprehensive, and that pronunciations are approximate at best due to the complex tonal character of spoken Chinese.

PINYIN SOUND EQUIVALENTS

    **c** – *ts* as in *its* (example: Cui = "Tsway")
    **q** – *ch* as in *chin* (example: Qinghai = "Ching-High")
    **x** – *sh* as in *sheet* (example: Xinjiang = "Shin-jee-ahng")
    **z** – *ds* as in *hands* (example: Zigong = "Dsih-Gong")
    **zh** – *j* as in *John* (example: Zhang Xing = "Jahng Shing")

# PROLOGUE

# STRANGER IN A STRANGE BAND

This isn't your everyday gig.

Sure, in some respects it's just like any other arena rock concert. I'm on stage playing electric guitar in a cavernous auditorium packed with keyed-up fans. The singer is strutting his stuff beneath a spotlight at center stage, looking rakish in his designer shades. Five other longhaired guys round out the band. The second guitarist unleashes a patented power-pop solo, face contorted in a classic rocker's grimace. Banks of stage lights flash blue-white-green as the drummer launches into the obligatory ham-fisted drum break, black tresses flying, arms a blur. The audience is eating it up.

You might think we were playing in Indianapolis or Topeka—until you notice the frowning guys in green military officers' uniforms studying us intently from side stage. It's not your typical rock concert crowd, either—no Mohawked slam-dancers or leather-clad rocker chicks in sight, but plenty of little old ladies, toddlers, and working-class blokes. The audience seems strangely subdued for a rock show. Between songs, the singer chats up the crowd. I can't understand a word he's saying.

The next song, our grand finale, commences with a lush keyboard intro, followed by soft guitar chords. Stage lights bathe the band in a rich carmine glow. The singer raises his microphone and begins crooning an incomprehensible lyric, something about "Ma Sushi." The audience murmurs in recognition and breaks into applause. The vocal line builds gradually in intensity, unfurling an oddly moving

*Dennis Rea with dancers, Chongqing Sports Arena 1991 (Tang Lei)*

singsong melody. I fumble around on my guitar, searching for the right notes as two lissome young women in flowing crimson silk dresses dance across the stage in front of me, waving matching red paper fans. The music swells to a climax, crunchy power chords echoing from the rafters as the keyboardist plays a triumphal theme. I coax quicksilver filaments of feedback out of my guitar in a closing flourish. The audience politely applauds, then rises en masse and heads quietly for the exits. A delegation of fresh-faced, smiling girls walks on stage and bestows bouquets of flowers on us.

Madison Square Garden it ain't—I'm a thousand miles up the Yangtze River in the ancient port city of Chongqing, China, just months after blood washed the paving stones of Tiananmen Square. I'm in town backing up Zhang Xing, a fading pop superstar who's on the comeback trail after spending several years in prison for being a pernicious influence on China's youth. We've just finished playing the band's signature tune, a risqué rock version of the Cultural Revolution classic "The Sun Is the Reddest, Chairman Mao Is the Dearest." The crowd was surprised to find a foreigner in Zhang Xing's band, but not half as surprised as me.

How on earth did an obscure Seattle-based experimental guitarist end up here?

# CHAPTER 1

# CHENGDU RUNDOWN

My music career in China got off to an inauspicious start when a taxi ran over my guitar an hour after I arrived in the country.

It was January 1989, and I had just touched down in the fog-bound inland city of Chengdu to begin a year of teaching English to Chinese graduate students. Ten months earlier I had accepted a position at Chengdu University of Science and Technology, where my fiancée, Anne Joiner, was participating in an academic exchange program. For Anne, who holds a degree in China Studies, the teaching assignment in Chengdu was a dream come true. For me, an idiosyncratic guitarist with a modest niche in the tiny Seattle experimental music scene, it was little more than a working vacation in an exotic locale.

I knew about three words of Chinese and had never had more than a passing interest in China before meeting Anne. Indeed, if our paths hadn't crossed, I might never have ventured across the Pacific to this day. Setting aside love interests, I had plenty of good reasons not to disappear overseas for a year, for I was making steady progress as a musician and was in no shape financially to take a teaching position that would pay me the equivalent of US$25 a week. Yet I had a strong presentiment that going to China would somehow prove to be a fortuitous move, even if it meant putting my music career on hold, so I shrugged off my misgivings and took the job.

In the months leading up to my departure, I spent much of my time reading up on China to better understand what I was getting into. I gained an appreciation for Chinese art and architecture, attended a reading by visiting Chinese poets, and immersed myself in traditional Chinese music, which happily resonated with my own musical sensibility. The more I learned, the more fascinated I became with the labyrinthine drama that is Chinese history—the stirring revolutionary movements, the sublime artistic achievements, the ineffable profundity of Taoism and other Chinese worldviews. By the time January rolled around I was eager to experience all of this for myself in Chengdu, the 2,500-year-old crossroads of storied Shu.

My adopted home was the political and cultural capital of Sichuan, China's most populous province with more than 120 million inhabitants at the time—roughly half the population of the United States living in an area the size of Texas. Two thousand years ago, what is now Sichuan was part of the independent state of Shu, one of the Three Kingdoms immortalized in Chinese literature and song. The classical poet Du Fu wasn't exaggerating when he wrote that "the road to Shu is more difficult than the road to heaven"; for centuries, travelers could only reach the mountain-girt Sichuan Basin by way of rugged, bandit-ridden defiles or a harrowing upstream boat journey through the fearsome Three Gorges of the Yangtze.

Sequestered at the western periphery of imperial jurisdiction, Sichuan's geographical isolation engendered a unique Chinese subculture with a distinct dialect and artistic traditions, extending all the way back to the Bronze Age Sanxingdui culture. Its people were famously resistant to outside rule and periodically rose up in rebellion against the imperial court. Even today, many residents consider themselves Sichuanese first and Chinese second.

The city of Chengdu sits astride the coffee-colored Jinjiang River at the western edge of the Chengdu Plain, a flat expanse of fertile farmland and rice paddies spread out beneath the soaring Snowy Mountains that form the eastern rampart of the Tibetan Plateau. A vital regional trade and transportation hub, Chengdu is the last major outpost of Chinese culture before one reaches the remote frontier uplands to the west, an area that is historically, ethnically, and geographically a part of Tibet. During my stay, Tibetans from isolated mountain villages were commonly seen hawking medicinal herbs, silver bracelets, and the hacked-off paws of endangered tigers and bears on the city's sidewalks.

Blessed with extraordinary agricultural wealth, the Chengdu area has long been the envy of less fortunate Chinese living in dirt-poor provinces like Shaanxi and Guizhou, hence its poetic sobriquet, the Land of Abundance. This fabled plenitude is due not only to the mild climate and nature's provenance, but also to the ingenuity of prefectural governor Li Bing, who in 250 BCE constructed one of the world's first large-scale irrigation systems to harness the torrents rushing down from the heights of the Snowy Mountains. In ancient times these wayward watercourses wandered capriciously across the plain, bringing untold grief to local villagers. Li Bing's innovative waterworks made possible a stable agricultural society, and subsequent extensions of his network of canals have carried sustenance to more than 8 million acres of Sichuan.

Whatever romantic notions I harbored of China as a land of poetry and watercolor landscapes were dashed upon my arrival in Chengdu, a booming metropolis of more than 3 million souls in 1989. The late-evening view from the taxi window revealed a society in the throes of a messy transition from a centrally planned socialist system to a market-driven economy, a confused patchwork quilt of old and new. As the taxi hurtled recklessly down dark rural byways in sticky fog, the driver now and then switching on his headlights to pin a startled bicyclist in the glare, I marveled at the bizarre incongruities produced by China's recent economic boom. Water buffaloes shared the road with swerving minibuses, bamboo groves reflected the flickering light of TV sets, and ageless rice paddies encircled sleek office towers housing brand-new import-export enterprises.

By all appearances, China was enjoying unprecedented prosperity. The country's living standard had risen dramatically in the decade since paramount leader Deng Xiaoping launched his bold economic-reform policies, a resurgence that was especially evident in Deng's native Sichuan, where many of his free-market innovations were first put into practice. Consumer goods were available as never before: Japanese-made TVs, video players, and boom-boxes proliferated, Marlboro cigarettes were essential status symbols for an emergent class of independent entrepreneurs, motorcycles were fast replacing the once-ubiquitous bicycle, and Maxwell House instant coffee was now the beverage of choice among *nouveau-riches* sophisticates. In my ignorance I had imagined that my electric guitar would be the only such instrument in town, but I would be happily mistaken.

Although my reading had led me to half-expect a repressive police state, China's newfound affluence appeared to have brought a corresponding relaxation of ideological and moral orthodoxy. The monochromatic blue uniforms of the Mao era had largely vanished, replaced by jeans and brightly colored print dresses. Cosmetics were making a comeback, hemlines were rising, and discos were all the rage, though ballroom dancing of the sort your grandmother enjoyed was about as racy as things got. The revolutionary anthems of yore had been abandoned in favor of Western pop staples like "Hello" and "Hotel California"; communist heroes such as the model soldier Lei Feng had yielded to Rambo and Tom "Top Gun" Cruise; and officers of the People's Liberation Army (PLA) were more likely to bum a cigarette than force you to write a self-criticism. Foreign-language bookstores attracted crowds of students eager to read translations of Steinbeck and Poe and biographies of industrialist heroes like Lee Iacocca. Cosmopolitan-minded youths gathered daily in a park near the Jinjiang Hotel to practice their English with foreign tourists, hungry for glimpses of a world that for decades had lain hidden behind a wall of impenetrable propaganda. But as events would soon prove, these outward manifestations of openness concealed a deep schism within Chinese society that was being steadily widened by spiraling inflation and public outrage over rampant corruption and the renewed stratification of Chinese society.

My white-knuckle taxi ride came to a merciful halt at the university gate, from which the ornamented rooflines of the older campus buildings were dimly visible in the dense fog. I got out and asked the uniformed gatekeeper for directions to the foreign teachers' lodgings, leaning my guitar against the taxi while I struggled to make myself understood in mangled Chinese.

Moments later I heard the taxi shift into reverse, followed by a soft thud. I turned just in time to see the vehicle's rear wheel spinning on top of my guitar, shredding its flimsy nylon case to tatters. Too stunned to berate the driver, I shouldered the damaged instrument and shelled out the requested 40 *renminbi* fare. I later learned that 20 RMB would have been a princely sum.

As it turned out, the taxi's wheel miraculously spared my guitar's vital parts. The instrument was still playable, though it now looked like someone had run over it with a lawnmower. Little did I suspect that the battered axe would be my key to musical adventures beyond my wildest imaginings.

# CHAPTER 2

# Anguish as a Second Language

My first weeks in Chengdu were not happy ones, and I often regretted my rash decision to take up the expatriate life. I couldn't help feeling like an ignorant interloper in Anne's sphere of interest, and though I'd taken a crash course in Mandarin Chinese before leaving Seattle, I couldn't speak the language to save my life. It didn't help that most people in Chengdu spoke the Sichuanese dialect, rendering my few Chinese lessons moot.

The weather was endlessly wet and gloomy; indeed, a local joke had it that Sichuanese dogs bark not at the moon but at the rarely seen sun. A thick pall of mist and particulate pollution obscured the city day and night, limiting visibility to a few hundred meters. Citizens had to do without central heating in this part of China, and even multiple layers of thick sweaters, worn indoors and out, failed to ward off the penetrating winter chill. We spent a lot of time huddled close to the ineffectual space heater in our frigid apartment.

In stark contrast to the tourist brochures' evocations of a charming "brocade city," I found Chengdu's urban landscape downright Dickensian at first. Austere Soviet-style housing blocks had swallowed up much of the surrounding farmland, and the celebrated hibiscus-clad city walls of old were now a series of expressways girdling the city with concentric rings of roaring traffic. Parks and riverside promenades, pounded bare of vegetation by untold millions of heels, turned into slurries of mud during the frequent downpours. On the rare occasions when the rain let up, dust raised by round-the-clock construction blended with coal smoke and nameless industrial effluents to cloak the city in an opaque miasma that doubtless had the kings of bygone Shu wheezing in their tombs. The last remaining precincts of oblique, narrow lanes and two-story timbered houses were fast disappearing to make room for frowning cement high-rises and thoroughfares lacking any sense of human scale, the price of a hopelessly overpopulated China's fervent embrace of modernity. I bicycled around town with a sinking feeling, wondering what on earth had possessed me to sentence myself to a year in such a dreary, polluted burg.

Yet as the weeks passed and I slowly found my place in the community, another Chengdu emerged, a city of leafy lanes and hidden teahouses where blue-suited elders passed humid afternoons sipping cups of fragrant jasmine tea grown in the nearby foothills. In spite of the many unsightly defacements wreaked in the name of progress, Chengdu remained one of China's more appealing cities, possessed of a relaxed civility and down-to-earth provincial charm that I later found to be largely absent in the manic metropolises of the eastern seaboard. And unlike most Chinese cities at that time, which shut down after dark as if under curfew, Chengdu boasted an active nightlife, with restaurants and bars doing a brisk business into the wee hours, offering such chili pepper–laced local favorites as Pockmarked Granny's Bean Curd and the city's legendary fire-and-brimstone hot pots. As time passed I grew to love slowly bicycling home in the moist night air with a bellyful of *chaoshou* dumplings and tepid *Lüye* beer.

Chengdu University of Science and Technology (Chengdu KeJi Daxue, or "KeDa" (kuh dah) for short) provided us with a small two-room apartment on the top floor of a residence hall reserved for foreign teachers and researchers. The building had been dubbed the "Panda Palace" by locals, who felt its occupants were every bit as pampered as the precious Sichuan mammal. Our accommodations were nothing to brag about but were obscenely luxurious by the local standards of the day, boasting such unheard-of amenities as a

*Chengdu street scene, 1991 (Spike Mafford)*

private sit-down toilet, a refrigerator, a television (all propaganda, all the time), and even an intermittently functioning washing machine. Our students would stare wide-eyed at these exotic treasures whenever they came to visit, accustomed as they were to sharing closet-size dorm rooms and malodorous public lavatories. Even the university president didn't merit the comforts lavished on foreign teachers to entice them to work in China.

Lest anyone think that we lived in the lap of luxury, it's worth mentioning that a visiting American architect once commented that the Panda Palace was very well preserved for a 30-year-old building, not realizing that it had been built just 5 years earlier. Power outages were commonplace, the faucets ran brown when they ran at all, and in winter the barren concrete rooms were cold as a tomb. The sticky summer months brought squadrons of ravenous mosquitoes and Mothra-class flying cockroaches. At intervals our mentally-ill neighbor would bellow through the night like a wounded elephant seal. But life was reasonably pleasant otherwise, enhanced by a profusion of fabulous, dirt-cheap Sichuanese cuisine and the welcome camaraderie of the foreign community.

Our fellow Panda Palace occupants were a polyglot crew of American teachers and Fulbright scholars, Soviet scientists, British Council careerists, and the odd Italian researcher, Canadian lecturer, and German backpacker. Even our Chinese hosts knew better than to house us with the missionary contingent that lived across campus, whose ministrations they barely tolerated in exchange for getting unpaid English instructors. Some of the more paranoid among the foreign residents actually examined the fixtures in their apartments for evidence of hidden surveillance devices, fearing communist spies. But who needed expensive high-tech gadgets when you had the *fuwuyuan*, or housekeepers, to monitor your every move? The *fuwuyuan* held keys to each of the foreigners' apartments and had a habit of barging in on tenants a split second after they knocked on the door. Privacy was an unthinkable privilege in crowded China, and the resentful university staff never missed an opportunity to invade the foreigners' living spaces and rummage through our belongings. Over the years a few startled teachers were even caught *in flagrante delicto* during unannounced *fuwuyuan* "raids."

Before long I settled into a routine at KeDa, teaching English in the daytime and hosting long bull sessions with students in our apartment at night under the pretense of "office hours." The university's Foreign Languages Department had assigned me classes in conversation, reading, and composition, based on decades-old textbooks that had cleared the gauntlet of government censors. I was acutely self-conscious due to my lack of formal teaching credentials—I had bluffed my way into the job, being a mere high school graduate—but I soon learned that my students were even more discomfited than I was. Most of them had never met a foreigner before walking into my classroom. They stared at me in wide-eyed wonder as though I were a Sasquatch.

When the semester got underway in February, I showed up for my first class gripped by anxiety, desperately hoping that I'd be up to the task of delivering a coherent lesson. I tried my best to project an aura of composure, smiling and greeting each student in turn as they filed into the classroom and took their places at the beat-up desks. My charges were graduate students in such fields as plastics, chemistry, structural engineering, and—fittingly for a province famed for its extensive waterworks—hydrology, many of whom would go on to work on the controversial Three Gorges Dam that would soon inundate that magnificent and historic stretch of the Yangtze. Males outnumbered females by about three to one. In most cases the students were studying English not by choice but by university directive, for command of the language of commerce was now considered essential to China's technological advancement. Their only previous foreign-language experience had been with Russian, a legacy of the erstwhile alliance of the now-estranged communist giants.

At our first meeting, I explained to my students that it was a departmental custom to adopt an English name and inquired if anybody already had one. Not a single student spoke up, so I suggested that they either choose a name before next week's class or select one from a list I would bring. The next time we met, I again asked the class for their English names and again met with blank silence. It looked like I would have to spend the entire class period assigning names instead of teaching useful language skills. But then, on a sudden hunch, I directly asked a random student if he'd chosen an English name; he promptly replied with "Robert." I then queried each student in turn and discovered that all but two had already picked names, but not one of them had summoned the nerve to speak up first. It dawned on me that in a society where going unnoticed was a critical survival tactic, getting my students to participate in class was going to be quite a challenge.

And what names they chose! Among the more entertaining monikers were Sweet, Snow, Roll, Hunter (after a lesser American TV action hero), Stranger, Lobster, Reagan, and even Dukakis. Not surprisingly, Dukakis evinced a keen interest in U.S. politics. Although his namesake had been soundly defeated in the recent presidential election, the Chinese Dukakis had not lost faith and assured me that his role model was certain to prevail in 1992.

Most audacious of all was the young man who dubbed himself God. I still treasure his handwritten self-introduction:

> My name is God, I live in Chongqing, China with my family. I specialize in automatic control theory. I want to go to foreign country to study, but it is very difficulty for Chinese to other country, because my country is poor now, I think my country will become very power.

The omniscient God would prove prophetic in this last observation. Not so amusing was the case of the unfortunate fellow who'd been christened "Jim's Bad Joke" by a jaded foreign teacher named Jim. Despite the best efforts of other teachers to persuade him to adopt a different name, Jim's Bad Joke adamantly refused, invoking the Chinese custom of unquestioning acquiescence to one's teachers.

Despite my inexperience and the deplorable conditions—dank, unheated, and unlit classrooms, broken windows, students un-self-consciously hawking and spitting on the floor—an easy rapport soon developed between me and my charges, and a little English actually got taught in the bargain.

While my students struggled with their participles, I received daily lessons in cultural dislocation. My attempts at humor fell flat, my cultural references went over the students' heads, and my insistence on their active participation in class paralyzed them. I quickly learned that most of these young people had never had a teacher ask their opinion or encourage them to come up with creative, independent solutions to scholastic problems.

This became all too apparent when several of my composition students turned in writing assignments that they had obviously copied verbatim from a standard textbook. Two even chose identical source material. I was taken aback at their audacity; did they really think I wouldn't see through their sudden mastery of vocabulary and syntax? Angered at this transparent deception, I disallowed the papers and sternly reprimanded the plagiarists. Strangely, they seemed not to understand why I was upset.

The next day a senior school official drew me aside and urged me to give the offenders passing grades. When I protested that the students had committed plagiarism, she patiently explained that the Chinese do not prize originality for its own sake but are encouraged to borrow freely from their betters. After all, who would presume to think that they could improve on the works of the masters? I later learned that this attitude carried over into the musical sphere as well. It's often impossible to identify the composers of classic Chinese musical works, for compositions were commonly based on anonymous folk melodies of indeterminate origin that were subsequently refined by later generations of nameless musicians.

Naturally, an educational system centered on rote learning and the parroting of memorized texts would seem to be at odds with Western notions of creativity and independent thinking. But while this approach has sometimes been taken to absurd extremes, as in the mindless follow-the-leader sloganeering of the Red Guards during the Cultural Revolution, one should always be careful not to judge one culture by the standards of another.

On a drizzly March afternoon about two months after my arrival, I answered a knock at my apartment door to find a group of earnest-looking students shuffling nervously outside. When I asked what they wanted, a thin fellow in a threadbare sport coat explained in halting English that they represented the university's guitar club.

Anne had told me that such a club existed, but I had not yet come in contact with any of its members. The interpreter went on to say that the head of the Foreign Languages Department had told them about the American electric guitarist who was teaching at KeDa, and they wanted to hear me play. Flattered, I responded that I'd be happy to oblige, but unfortunately I had only been able to bring a tiny headphone monitor with me for private practice. I could never have traveled with a full-size amplifier, as heavily laden with textbooks and personal effects as I'd been, and the chances of needing one had seemed rather remote anyway. The young guitarists quickly assured me that they had already borrowed an amplifier for my use.

The delegation lingered awkwardly at my doorstep. It gradually dawned on me that they expected a recital that very instant. Since I didn't seem to have any choice in the matter, I compliantly grabbed my guitar and followed the club members to a freezing, barely lit classroom where I was surprised to find about 25 people silently awaiting me. This was the first time I experienced a situation that would become all too familiar during my stay in China, where any minor occasion involving a foreigner was somehow escalated into an Event.

After a fumbling self-introduction, I plugged my taxi-scarred guitar into the cheap amp provided by the students, tuned up, and gave a brief demonstration of my playing skills. The students stared intently as I played a jazz ballad and a few of my own tunes, hampered by finger-numbing cold. I found the intense scrutiny unnerving. For the life of me, I couldn't tell if the audience was enjoying the performance or not, but as soon as I finished they eagerly crowded around to ask questions and inspect my guitar. I had evidently passed muster.

# CHAPTER 3

# ANATOMY OF A GUITARIST

I first took up the guitar at age nine, inspired by guitarist Mike Nesmith of the Monkees after hearing their hit "Last Train to Clarksville." It was later revealed that the band didn't even play the instruments on their early albums; the signature Monkees sound was actually the work of a group of anonymous studio musicians. So much for role models.

My parents were understandably dubious about my musical aspirations and resisted repeated entreaties to buy me a guitar. My mother finally softened one day at the sight of me mournfully strumming a cigar box strung with rubber bands. When I came home from school the next afternoon, I found a brand-new $10 Montgomery Ward "Airline" acoustic guitar in my bedroom.

My first formal lesson was with a journeyman guitar instructor at Peate's Music in my hometown of Utica, New York. The teacher burst out laughing at my first attempt to sound a note on my new guitar, dealing a crushing blow to my self-esteem. I left humiliated and vowed never to take another lesson with him.

My next guitar teacher was more considerate but something of a moldy fig, feeding me a steady musical diet of nursery tunes and Christmas carols. Like most kids my age, I wanted to play songs by my favorite rock bands, and I soon dreaded going to class. A few months into *Alfred's Basic Guitar Course*, I bailed out on my lessons and even stopped playing the guitar altogether for a couple of years. Although I eventually found teachers who were more sympathetic

*The author in Chengdu, 1991 (Xiao Quan)*

to my interests, my early guitar studies left me with a lasting distrust of orthodox musical education.

While I shared my peers' enthusiasm for the Beatles and other pop groups of the day, by an early age I had already acquired a taste for "weird" music. I remember being enchanted by my sister Susan's cast-off single of Nat King Cole singing the exotica curiosity "Hajji Baba," and by the otherworldly piping that accompanied appearances by the Sea Hag in Popeye cartoons. Another unwitting benefactor in my musical development was my Uncle Billy, a classical music enthusiast who unloaded boxes of unwanted record club bonus LPs on family members every Christmas. One such shipment included a record of abstract electronic music by avant-garde composer John Cage; I delighted in its sheer sonic audacity, much to my parents' dismay. Hearing experimental works like this and György Ligeti's psychotropic soundtrack to *2001: A Space Odyssey* proved to be formative events in my musical development, as I learned to accept "nonmusical" sounds without prejudice.

Like so many other teenage guitarists of my generation, I flipped for the Who, Jimi Hendrix, and the Allman Brothers. After a while

I grew my hair long, dusted off my neglected Airline acoustic, and started playing again, this time for keeps. Although I resumed guitar lessons with a friendly neighborhood rocker named Don Wolfe, I found reading music to be a chore and soon took to playing by ear, a decision that has since proven to be both an advantage and a liability. At age 15 I formed a basement band with some high school buddies and wrote my first songs. As my musical tastes continued to evolve, I quickly grew bored with basic blues-based rock and put in long hours mastering dissonant chords and unusual time signatures, influenced by eccentric progressive rock outfits like King Crimson and Soft Machine. I identified strongly with these groups' adventurousness and willingness to embrace new sounds. Around the same time, my older brother Woody, an erstwhile beatnik who lived on the West Coast in Seattle, introduced me to the modern jazz of Miles Davis, John Coltrane, and Ornette Coleman, fueling my growing interest in improvisation. I also began investigating the experimental classical music of composers such as Penderecki and Stockhausen.

In the early 1970s I formed the trio Zuir with bassist Norm Peach and drummer Dan Zongrone, as a vehicle for my ambitious instrumental rock compositions. With our lengthy explorations of psychedelic sound effects and convoluted rhythms, Zuir was in a league of its own in country rock–saturated Utica. Realizing that our material would never fly in the local redneck boogie bars, Zuir opted for the do-it-yourself approach, renting small theaters and promoting our own concerts. While in retrospect much of our music was embarrassingly immature, it was rather outré in its context and soon attracted a devoted following in the Utica area. So fervently did the band members believe in Zuir that we all chose to skip college in favor of taking a shot at success in the music world. In an act of astonishing naiveté, we decided to relocate to distant Seattle at age 18, partly because my brother Woody had offered to manage the band, partly to get as far away as possible from the cultural and economic backwater of Utica. In October 1975 we stuffed our band equipment into a beat-up International Travelall and made the long drive to Seattle with just a few hundred dollars in our collective pocket.

We soon discovered that Seattle audiences were no more receptive to our peculiar music than those in Utica. A half-year later we drove back to our hometown in defeat. The band broke up shortly thereafter, largely because of my stubborn refusal to play music with more commercial appeal. But at least Zuir had the distinction of being one of the first East Coast rock bands to move to Seattle in search of pay dirt, almost 20 years before the grunge revolution precipitated hundreds of similar migrations.

Depressed at the demise of Zuir and determined not to be mired in the tar pit that was 1970s Utica, I moved back to Seattle in 1978 with the intention of attending music school. Just a few weeks after I arrived on the West Coast, however, news reached me that another Utica musician, Craig Wuest, was enjoying spectacular success in Germany and wanted me to join him there to collaborate on a record. Craig had been one of the earliest electronic musicians in Utica and arguably the first in the city to own a synthesizer. Heavily influenced by German experimentalists such as Tangerine Dream and Kraftwerk, Craig had struck up a correspondence with synthesizer legend Klaus Schulze that led him to make a series of albums in Germany under the name Earthstar. I was one of several old Utica mates invited to participate in the project. Since the prospect of making a record with international music luminaries was an offer I couldn't refuse, I dropped my plans to attend music school and instead spent half a year in the countryside near Hannover working on Earthstar sessions, which were eventually released on Germany's Sky label in the early 1980s. Although Earthstar was little more than an obscure footnote to the "krautrock" phenomenon at the time, we were astonished to find one of our records reissued on CD 20 years later and hailed as "a synthesizer music classic," though I personally wouldn't be that charitable.

Back in Seattle after the Earthstar sessions, I came in contact with another electronic composer, Kerry Leimer, who had made a name for himself with several self-produced LPs on his independent Palace of Lights label. Like composer/conceptualist Brian Eno, Leimer was fascinated with the possibilities of "systems" music, where the process by which the music is made is at least as important as the resulting musical content—hence album titles like *Closed System Potentials*. Leimer had recently formed a loose group called Savant that provided a more grounded setting for his lofty compositional ideas. I joined Savant in 1982 and contributed to the LP *The Neo-Realist (at Risk)*, described by *Downbeat* magazine as "pan-ethnic techno-dub music." At about this time I also met composer Jeff Greinke, with whom I would eventually travel to China—but that's a tale for later in this book.

Looking to broaden my horizons after a failed first marriage, I moved to New York City in 1983 and hovered around the edges of the experimental and improvised music communities. The vaunted Downtown creative music scene centered on Bill Laswell, John Zorn, and other fierce innovators was then in full flower, and I was fortunate to take in a great deal of imaginative music and rub shoulders with many notable composers, instrumentalists, and artists of all stripes. But after three years of slumming on the grim, crack-ridden Lower East Side, the clean, green environs of the Pacific Northwest once again beckoned. In late 1986 I bounced back to Seattle, where I was delighted to find that the adventurous music community had grown considerably in my absence. I jumped back into the scene with renewed vigor and over the next few years played in numerous avant-rock bands and improvising aggregates with names like Particle Theory and Catabatics, in addition to co-organizing the fledgling Seattle Improvised Music Festival and writing about music in local publications.

It was during this period that I met and fell in love with my future wife, Anne, who would soon leave the country to take up her teaching position in Chengdu. After more than a dozen years of fits and starts, I was just beginning to hit my stride as a performing musician when Anne wrote from China with an offer of employment at her university. The proposal threw me into a quandary. I missed Anne terribly and was intrigued at the prospect of living in the alluring East, but I was afraid that it would be a mistake to walk away from my musical involvements now that I'd finally gained some traction. In the end, love and curiosity won out. Perhaps I would even find opportunities to play music publicly in China, unlikely as it seemed. Besides, it would only be for a year—or so I thought.

Just before I left for China, I was offered a studio gig by the producers of a locally produced feature film, *Shredder Orpheus*, a campy remake of the Greek myth featuring a skate-punk Orpheus who wielded a mean heavy-metal guitar, played on the soundtrack by yours truly. The session also featured composer Roland Barker and future REM and King Crimson drummer Bill Rieflin, who figure later in this story.

It was with this background in way-out jazz, left-field instrumental rock, free improvisation, and electronic space music that I showed up in ultraconservative China, where Andy Williams, John Denver, and cornball pianist Richard Clayderman were considered the cutting edge. I was a most unlikely candidate for the role of musical envoy, considering that my music had virtually no mass appeal and that I had all the stage presence of a meditating monk. Judging by the singularly unimaginative pop music then prevalent in China, there seemed to be little room for my brand of instrumental adventurism. I had brought my guitar basically to amuse myself and keep in practice, and had scant expectation of playing music publicly.

# CHAPTER 4

# SICHUAN BLUES

Among those present at my first impromptu performance for the university guitar club was a 34-year-old guitarist named Zhao Xiong. A slight, thoughtful man with a dashing Clark Gable mustache, Zhao Xiong evidently commanded a lot of respect within the surprisingly populous Chengdu guitar community, being one of several players touted by various factions as the city's "Number One" guitarist. One thing that set him apart from the crowd was his rare 12-string guitar, perhaps the only instrument of its kind in the region. And unlike most Chengdu guitarists, who specialized in either the Western classical repertoire or Mandarin pop songs, Zhao Xiong composed his own idiosyncratic, bluesy instrumental pieces.

Zhao Xiong's travails as a working musician were typical of Chinese players of his generation. As a teenager during the Cultural Revolution, the Chengdu native was sent to the provincial backwater of Dukou for "reeducation through labor" because of his parents' alleged bad class background. (After coming to power in 1949, the Chinese Communist Party established what amounted to a caste system based on a person's perceived class affiliations. Those pariahs who got shipped off to labor camps were lucky compared to the millions who were executed by the military or turned over to vengeful mobs, often with scant justification.)

The young Zhao Xiong spent the next few years shoveling scrap metal in the dismal industrial hellhole of Dukou. Physically and emotionally spent, he channeled his frustrations into music, learning the rudiments of guitar playing from a classical guitarist who lived nearby. When China's political situation relaxed somewhat after Mao's death in 1976, Zhao Xiong sought permission to move back to Chengdu but was rebuffed by government bureaucrats. He seemed fated for a life of hard labor, far from family and friends.

The ambitious young musician redoubled his efforts to master the guitar and made rapid progress. Eventually he gained enough confidence to do something nearly unthinkable at the time: He quit his *danwei*—the social/work unit to which each Chinese citizen was assigned, usually for life—to take up the highly uncertain calling of an independent musician. He made his way back to Chengdu in search of better opportunities but soon found that, without *danwei* membership or the required musicians' working papers, he was barred from playing professionally. Thwarted in his ambitions for the moment, he continued to hone his skills in his parents' tiny apartment and played the occasional private party. Around this time he met an English teacher from Minnesota who generously gave him his trademark 12-string guitar. Unfortunately, Zhao Xiong permanently injured his right hand in an accident around this time and was

*Zhao Xiong with the author (Tang Lei)*

forced to abandon the classical guitar regimen for less demanding folk and pop music.

Zhao Xiong eventually overcame all these obstacles and regained his legal residency in Chengdu. He immediately joined a dancehall band that possessed the coveted musicians' working papers. (Professional musicians were required to obtain the Chinese equivalent of a cabaret card and display it on their persons when playing. In a uniquely Chinese twist, the government issued the cards only to groups, not to individuals.) The newly credentialed guitarist was soon working seven nights a week in a trashy disco, regurgitating bland Taiwanese pop ballads with mind-numbing repetition.

By the time I met Zhao Xiong he was only too happy to expand his musical horizons. Shortly after my "audition" for the KeDa guitar club, he dropped by my apartment and asked me to take him on as a guitar student. Beyond the fact that he obviously possessed musical talent, I found Zhao Xiong a very agreeable fellow, so I consented to give him weekly lessons at my apartment. Our teacher-student relationship quickly evolved into a valued friendship. I was delighted to find someone who was eager to learn my quirky compositions, and our partnership led to our performing and recording together on many occasions. He was also one of the very few people I met in China who could understand my pathetic pidgin Chinese. (He spoke not a word of English himself.)

Zhao Xiong also put me in contact with the larger musical community outside the university. As president of the informal Chengdu Guitar Association—there were in fact three such cabals headed by rival guitarists—Zhao Xiong regularly organized guitar concerts throughout the local area. I took part in several of these events, playing at schools, the Worker's Cultural Palace, and even a textile factory in the countryside (the prosaically named Factory No. 7448). Some of these shows were surprisingly large happenings attended by hundreds of people and offering a veritable smorgasbord of guitar music, ranging from earnest folksingers to classical guitarists to, ahem, the American Guitarist. My relationship with the Chengdu Guitar Association worked to everyone's advantage—audiences were titillated to hear a real, live foreign guitar player, I found a welcome outlet for performing my music, and the Association gained major face in the bargain.

These early concert appearances forced me to develop an eclectic solo repertoire that included moody jazz ballads, up-tempo rhythmic workouts, and loose interpretations of *pipa* (Chinese lute) and *erhu* (two-stringed fiddle) classics. Not surprisingly, my guitar adaptations of Chinese songs proved a big hit with listeners. My decision to play Chinese traditional music was partly a gesture of respect for my hosts, partly a personal challenge, and partly a result of my growing interest in the music, much of which lends itself surprisingly well to the electric guitar. The scooped, sliding tones characteristic of the *erhu* and *guzheng* (horizontal zither) find parallels in the string-bending and bottleneck techniques employed by blues guitarists; for that matter, a large part of the Chinese traditional repertoire, built on pentatonic scales and suffused with a profound melancholia rooted in centuries of suffering, is strikingly similar in spirit, if not in structure, to rural American blues. Another aspect of Chinese music that appealed to me was its rhythmic flexibility; rather than being shackled to a rigid pulse like most Western fare, Chinese music is often marked by subtle fluctuations of tempo, allowing the player greater freedom of expression.

Encouraged by the warm audience response, I began to take more risks, cautiously introducing more dissonance and unorthodox playing techniques into my sets. To my surprise, demonstrations of feedback and weird sound effects proved to be perennial crowd-pleasers. While it would be a gross exaggeration to say that I won over the broad Chinese masses to unconventional music, the audiences that I did reach were unfailingly curious, attentive, and engaged, if somewhat baffled. I was also struck by the remarkable diversity of attendees, ranging from small children to factory workers to Party officials, a refreshing contrast to the hipper-than-thou exclusivity of audiences back in Seattle.

Though audiences were generally enthusiastic, the circumstances under which I played were another thing altogether. I thought I had put up with less than ideal conditions in the States—apathetic sound engineers, boorish club owners, toxic clouds of cigarette smoke—but none of this prepared me for the realities of playing in China in 1989.

Wintertime was especially trying. To conserve money and resources, the Chinese government had decreed that public buildings in southern China go without central heating despite the penetrating midwinter chill. This meant playing shows in sub-freezing temperatures, cocooned in a half-dozen sweaters and exhaling billows of breath vapor. Playing an instrument well demands a certain degree of digital dexterity even under the best of circumstances, but in Chengdu the biting cold all but crippled my fingers, making it devilishly difficult to get through even the simplest musical numbers. I took to furiously rubbing my hands together, burying them in my pockets or armpits, gripping cups of hot tea to the point of pain, and even running laps around the building before taking the stage.

Finding serviceable equipment was another chronic dilemma. Although dependable brand-name music gear is now widely available in most Chinese cities, in 1989 a musician had to settle for whatever third-rate supplies could be obtained locally. As a guitarist, I found it especially difficult to obtain decent amplifiers. Most of the Chinese-made amps of the day were woefully inadequate and sounded dreadful even on the rare occasions when they worked properly. Sometimes it seemed as though people actually preferred the sound of ruptured speakers; indeed, most people were so inured to the highly amplified government propaganda that erupted incessantly from broken loudspeakers in public places—broadsides against "rightism" and the like—that they could sleep peacefully right through the din.

Most of my equipment woes were the result of a simple semantic misunderstanding. In Western musical parlance, the term "amplifier" normally denotes amplification devices designed for individual instruments; for example, a bass amp for a bass guitar. But in China the equivalent term, *yinxiang,* is used both for instrument amps and for much larger public-address systems, causing endless confusion for foreign musicians. Again and again I would request a basic guitar amplifier, only to find myself presented with a stadium-size PA system.

The simple act of plugging in one's equipment could also be quite an escapade. Onstage power outlets were often bizarre Rube Goldberg contraptions cobbled together from exposed wires and swatches of tape. Power outages in mid-show were a matter of course. When the power *was* functioning, the music was frequently obliterated by an enervating electrical buzz. Replacing faulty equipment was an exercise in patience. On one occasion when I badly needed a new guitar cable, I went to a shop that sold both electric guitars and amplifiers, only to find that they didn't carry the cables that connect the two. When I asked the surly clerk where I could purchase a cable, he laughed in my face and told me that I would have to make one myself out of parts. Of course, the parts were only available at two different shops located at opposite ends of town—one that sold wire and another that sold plugs. Because the manufacture of wire fell under the jurisdiction of one government ministry and the making of plugs under another, the two components couldn't legally be sold in the same state sales outlet. When I finally managed to track down the necessary parts a week later, I had to recruit someone with a soldering iron to help me weld them together.

Zhao Xiong's rivals in the triumvirate of Chengdu "Number One" guitarists included Chen Minggui, a professional player who'd made a similar transition from classical to electric guitarist, and the teenaged Zhou Di, a conservatory student and aspiring heavy metal rocker. Like Zhao Xiong and so many other Chinese musicians at that time, both guitarists worked the local disco circuit and dreamed of studying music in the United States.

A technically competent if unimaginative player, Chen Minggui constantly importuned me to intervene on his behalf with universities in the U.S., oblivious to my protestations that I didn't have the clout to influence institutional decisions. In a society where personal connections routinely supersede the law, many people found it hard to believe that things (usually) worked differently where I came from. Students routinely pressured foreign teachers to cajole visas from U.S. consular officials, which of course we were powerless to do. When the consulate inevitably rejected their applications, some students reacted as though we had personally betrayed them.

Unlike Chen Minggui and Zhao Xiong, the younger Zhou Di was too proud to curry my favor. A student of traditional *erhu* music at Sichuan Music Conservatory, he had long since taken up the banner of Western hard rock in the testosterone-laced tradition of Deep Purple and Van Halen. Too young to remember the depredations of the Cultural Revolution, Zhou Di was typical of a new generation of media-savvy Chinese youth who were far more worldly and self-confident than their traumatized parents. He grew out his hair, affected a rocker's pout, and ran with a fast crowd of budding hoodlums. But he was also a genuinely talented guitarist, gifted with more fire and finesse than older rivals who came up playing classical and folk music. He would later become a significant player in the Beijing rock scene of the 1990s as leader of the successful band Compass.

When not buckling down to his studies, Zhou Di could be found moonlighting in hotel discos with *Hei Ma* ("Black Horse"), an early Chengdu rock band that managed to slip a few head-bangers into their otherwise innocuous sets of Chinese pop hits. The group had a wealthy patron in Mr. Zhao, a flamboyant department-store magnate reputed to be Chengdu's first millionaire. The extravagant Mr.

Zhao lavished expensive equipment on his pet band that other local musicians could only dream of, and booked them a lucrative regular gig at his glitzy disco. I sat in with Black Horse at the disco on a couple of occasions, followed by nightlong bouts of ostentatious feasting and toasts at Mr. Zhao's expense. The embodiment of the reform-era entrepreneurial success story, this modern-day Mandarin thought nothing of spending on a night of partying what most Chinese people earned in a year, epitomizing the resurgence of class consciousness in a once fiercely egalitarian China.

# CHAPTER 5

# THE GREAT WALL OF SOUND

Accustomed as I was to the obsessive categorization of music in the West, I was continually struck by the almost surreal stylistic diversity of musical events in China. It wasn't unusual for a single concert to include Western classical, Chinese traditional, folk, and pop music on the same bill—imagine a gig shared by Megadeth, Joan Baez, Yo-Yo Ma, and Ravi Shankar and you'll get the picture. The same was true of Chinese television, where variety shows consistently scored the highest ratings. Unlike audiences in the U.S., the Chinese listeners I encountered were unusually receptive to the full cornucopia of musical offerings, while American listeners seemed to define themselves more by what they don't like than by what they do.

Ever since the quarantine against Western cultural exports was partially lifted in the late 1970s, China had been flooded with unfamiliar foreign music. Consequently, listeners didn't have a clear idea of what was or wasn't hip. As a musician who has little patience for ephemeral, market-driven fashions, I found this tremendously liberating.

The more I spoke with people about music, the more aware I became of some of the fundamental differences between Eastern and Western musical thinking. As a case in point, each morning at dawn, students at our school would dutifully gather on the university grounds for regimented physical exercise, egged on by earsplitting loudspeakers barking *one! two! three! four!* to musical accompaniment. Something struck me as odd about the exercise tapes, but I couldn't put my finger on it at first. Then one day it finally dawned on me: The music, a Strauss waltz, was in triple meter—meaning its underlying rhythm was counted in units of three beats—yet the makers of the exercise tape had superimposed a four-beat count on the waltz, seemingly unaware that the two rhythmic patterns clashed. What registered instinctively as the "wrong" rhythm to my Western ears evidently was not at all apparent to these listeners, whose musical traditions are largely based on two-beat increments rather than groupings of three or four beats as in the West.

Musical improvisation was an especially challenging concept to get across to my listeners. Many people were surprised to hear that much of my playing was completely off the cuff and wondered why any musician would choose to jump without a parachute. Once common in Chinese music, improvisation had long since fallen out of practice, except in out-of-the-way areas where rural folk music traditions had survived intact. The devaluation of improvisation was nowhere more evident than in the state music academies, which focused almost exclusively on the rote reproduction of a handful of approved Chinese and European classical compositions. I'll venture that one reason why China's state-enforced musical orthodoxy allowed little leeway for personal interpretation is that improvisation is tantamount to independent thinking, precisely what any totalitarian government fears most.

Similarly, listeners often asked me to explain the "meaning" of a particular piece of music. The question is understandable when one considers that Chinese instrumental music historically has been either representative ("Moonlight in Spring Water"), programmatic ("Ambushed from All Sides"), or ceremonial, rather than being an abstract sonic event in its own right. But since most non-vocal music in the Western tradition has no specific message to convey or story to tell, I was invariably at a loss to assign meaning to the music I played.

In late spring I was invited to give a lecture on jazz at Sichuan Music Conservatory, the hub of music education in Southwest China and Tibet. Like most Chinese music schools at the time, the Sichuan conservatory enforced a strict diet of pre-twentieth-century Western classical chestnuts, so-called People's Music, and musty "national" tunes. Inside the conservatory gate stood a statue of official revolutionary composer Nie Er, a daily reminder of music's subservience to ideology. On campus, students smothered in thick sweaters put in long hours at the piano or *erhu* in dripping, inadequately lit practice rooms. Many Chinese viewed music as an avenue of escape from the crushing poverty and banality of their everyday lives, but only a tiny percentage of applicants successfully negotiated the bureaucratic maze to gain entrance to China's dozen or so conservatories. A lucky few might go on to be concert musicians and perhaps even travel abroad, but most would end up accepting poorly paid positions in provincial orchestras or remain at the conservatory training new generations of aspirants. Such was the lot of our friend Li, a talented pianist who well into middle age still clung tenaciously to her dream of entering Juilliard.

Much to the dismay of school officials, by the late 1980s more and more conservatory students were breaking ranks to seek careers in commercial pop music. The conservatory even instituted an evening curfew to deter students from moonlighting in disco bands for extra cash, but rebels like Zhou Di simply climbed over the campus walls after dark and slunk off to make a few precious bucks playing the latest Hong Kong pop tunes in tacky hotel ballrooms.

The otherwise moribund conservatory did boast a small cadre of avant-garde musicians centered on the composer He Xuntian. Winner of first prize at the 1984 All-China Music Competition, the ambitious He was known for devising an arcane method of composition that he termed "RD." Among his notable early works was the remarkable tone poem "Sounds of Nature," which employed traditional Chinese instruments in uncanny evocations of wind, thunder, and other natural sonic phenomena. Ironically, in a few years He Xuntian would largely abandon serious composition for a lucrative career as the progenitor of Chinese "new age" music.

At the time of my lecture at the conservatory, jazz was known only to a tiny circle of Chinese musicians and cognoscenti but was poised to make a comeback after nearly 40 years of tacit prohibition. Appropriately, China's first encounter with jazz came during Shanghai's vaunted "Jazz Age" of the 1920s and 30s, when visiting jazz stars such as trumpeter Buck Clayton performed for largely expatriate audiences in the city's foreign concessions. Local musicians soon embraced the imported genre, most famously the Peace Hotel Jazz Band, who played in that hotel's opulent ballroom. Filtered through jazz-influenced musicians such as Jin Huaizu ("Jimmy King") and the prolific composer Li Jinhui, echoes of jazz were audible in much of the popular and film music of the day.

Stigmatized as purveyors of a decadent foreign art form, Shanghai's jazz musicians were silenced by an insular Communist regime after the 1949 revolution. Jazz remained virtually nonexistent in China until its revival during the cultural thaw of the post-Mao era, when the now-elderly Peace Hotel Jazz Band resumed playing to packed houses in the expensively refurbished hotel ballroom on Shanghai's Bund. When Anne and I saw them perform in early 1989, the geriatric jazzmen served up an anemic variety of lounge music with little, if any, genuine improvising. Still, "real" jazz or not, the group was a big hit with the patrons, who showered the musicians with cash, drinks, and cartons of Marlboros between sets.

Jazz gained a small but enthusiastic following in the 1980s, fueled by the increasing availability of jazz recordings from abroad and renewed public exposure to expatriate jazz musicians. The first noteworthy statement from China's new jazz generation was the 1988 China Record Company release *Jazz in China* by pianist and composer Gao Ping, who passed through Anne's intensive English program the same year. Although only marginally jazz by most measures, this early effort was nevertheless significant for its spirit of openness and emphasis on improvisation. Remarkably, within just 10 years, China would produce a number of truly impressive jazz soloists and boast an acclaimed international jazz festival, raising the possibility that jazz, with its accommodating open structures, might hold the key to a truly democratic union of Chinese and other world musical traditions.

My lecture was attended primarily by young music students with a taste for foreign culture and ideas, most of them budding rockers with only a vague notion of what jazz was. I began to wonder why I had taken on the challenge of making jazz comprehensible to people who had never really listened to it. Faced with condensing the entire body of jazz history into a two-hour discussion, I decided to forgo theoretical analysis and let the music speak for itself, so I played the audience selected recordings covering a comprehensive range of jazz styles, adding a bit of spoken commentary.

Despite a faltering translation, the lecture went over well with most of the students. But during the question-and-answer session that followed I found myself challenged by the composer He Xuntian, who complained, "You've talked and talked, but you still haven't told us what jazz is." I sighed in frustration, tempted to trot out the old line "If you have to ask, you'll never know." I patiently explained that even jazz historians cannot agree on a single definition for jazz and that my examples had been deliberately chosen to underscore the plurality of jazz styles and approaches. When I posited that jazz was less a set of musical theorems than a way of thinking about music, He Xuntian scoffed, "Your answer is not really an answer." As remarkable a composer as he was, He Xuntian completely missed the point of jazz. Never was I so acutely aware of the inadequacy of words to describe music. It was difficult enough to discuss jazz with people who spoke my own language; how could I possibly explain to a Chinese musician the meaning of such subjective terms as "swing," "cool," and "in the pocket," or verbalize jazz's subtle nuances of feeling and expression?

To be sure, some of the younger musicians did seem to instinctively grasp the idea of jazz. One such player was the teenaged Yang Chenggang, a piano prodigy whose father headed the Keyboard Studies department at Sichuan Conservatory. Determined that his son should study at a conservatory in the U.S., Yang's father enrolled him in an English training program at KeDa, where Anne was among his teachers. The young pianist soon became a daily fixture at our apartment, chain-smoking and carrying on excitedly about jazz late into the night. We inevitably became musical collaborators, playing shaky renditions of old Errol Garner tunes in the new bars opening all over the city.

Yang was fortunate to have an unusually broad-minded father who'd amassed a singular library of classical and jazz records. The elder Yang enjoyed a privileged position at the conservatory, in part because of his glowing revolutionary credentials. Before the 1949 revolution, Yang Jr.'s grandmother had been a concubine of a notoriously oppressive Sichuan landlord. During her captivity she fell deeply in love with a peasant laborer and conceived his child. The landlord's retainers eventually discovered the woman's pregnancy, and the moment she delivered her infant son, he was seized and thrown into a well. Providentially, a local peasant witnessed the attempted drowning and rescued the boy who would become Yang Chenggang's father. Local villagers raised the child, keeping its parentage secret from the landlord. Years later, when the triumphant People's Liberation Army forcefully divested Sichuan's landlords of their holdings, Yang Sr. found himself elevated to the status of a revolutionary hero. In later life he airbrushed the details of his birth, and his son was completely unaware of the story, which I learned about from a family friend.

In an amusing sidebar to my jazz lecture, the conservatory's official English translator, a young woman named Zheng, asked if I would like to earn some extra money doing an English voice-over for a film being produced by Sichuan Television. I didn't really care about the money, but the project seemed like a fun diversion, so I accepted. A few days later Ms. Zheng and I pedaled our bicycles down to the TV studio for the taping session. She introduced me to her friend the director, and the three of us sat down to view the scenes I was about to dub. Only then did I learn that I had been hired to provide the voices of two black Africans! (I'm Irish by ancestry.)

The resourceful director was trying to make an easy buck turning a previously made propaganda film into a TV movie. The original government-produced footage documented a "goodwill" trip to Kenya by a Chinese engineering corps that oversaw the construction of a new sports stadium. The footage consisted mainly of construction and demolition scenes and shots of African and Chinese officials consulting each other over blueprints. Since the government had already picked up the tab for the film, the director was now cannibalizing it freely for his commercial project, re-sequencing scenes and overdubbing dialogue to match a contrived plot. My job was to dub English dialogue for the Kenyans. The filmmaker didn't seem to care that I was of a different race or that the Kenyans might not have been speaking English—this time, the old cliché that all foreigners look alike apparently rang all too true.

I did my best to come up with two dissimilar voices for my characters and gradually got the hang of synchronizing my vocal delivery with the moving images. The script itself was another thing, and I soon regretted my casual decision to narrate it sight-unseen. In the director's Sinocentric TV version of events, the African officials and construction workers were rendered as scheming scoundrels who'd tried to cheat their Chinese benefactors by inflating cost estimates. Of course the crooks were brought to justice in the end, and in the film's final scene the Africans were shown begging the paternalistic Chinese officials' forgiveness. (In the original footage, the Africans and Chinese were simply discussing construction methods.) Imagine my dismay at having been hoodwinked into reciting this offensive trash. But at least I fared better than my fellow KeDa English teacher Dani, who gullibly accepted an all-expenses-paid trip to tropical Xishuangbanna to act in a Chinese film, only to find herself cast as a foreign gang-rape victim.

A month later, on June 3, I delivered a second lecture at Sichuan Music Conservatory, this time a seminar on electric guitar technique for an audience made up chiefly of guitar players and aspiring rock-and-rollers. I demonstrated different playing styles and ways of expanding the guitar's tonal palette by using electronic effects, feedback, the tremolo bar, and objects inserted between the strings, even playing with chopsticks and a shoeshine brush. The seminar was a hit with the young players, giving me hope that this new generation of musicians would one day bring China into the modern world musically as well as economically. Little did anyone suspect that in a few short hours, events would occur that would reverberate throughout all of China, and indeed throughout the world.

# CHAPTER 6

# RED SCAR OVER CHINA

On 15 April 1989, my students excitedly informed me that onetime senior Communist Party leader Hu Yaobang had succumbed to a heart attack. Once pegged to succeed Deng Xiaoping as China's supreme leader, the relatively liberal Hu had been cashiered by Deng for his tacit support of pro-democracy demonstrations in Beijing and other cities in 1986, earning him martyrdom in the eyes of many students and intellectuals. As the news of Hu's death spread, spontaneous memorial gatherings materialized in cities throughout China, including Chengdu. This nationwide gesture of respect for the popular Hu was widely viewed as a rebuke to China's current leadership.

To everyone's surprise, the commemorative assemblies continued for days and steadily grew in size. Impassioned student leaders with megaphones held forth daily before sympathetic crowds, eulogizing the late Hu as the type of leader that China sorely needed. Before long the emboldened demonstrators were openly denouncing the Deng Xiaoping regime and blaming it for the institutionalized cancer of government corruption that was creating a dangerously polarized society of haves and have-nots. For while a privileged elite of private entrepreneurs and import-export wheeler-dealers were steadily enriching themselves in collusion with Communist Party insiders, most Chinese citizens continued to subsist on an annual income of roughly US$200 and could only dream of purchasing the latest consumer products on tantalizing display in trendy new shops.

The benefits of China's vaunted economic boom certainly didn't extend to my students, who led lives of sobering austerity. Three times daily the young academics would troop down to the campus commissary with their dented tin bowls for meals that made American prison fare seem like the chef's special at Delmonico's— gristly meat of indeterminate origin, pale, overcooked vegetables, and a couple of scoops of coarse rice that often concealed shards of tooth-shattering stone. Most of the students wore the same clothes to class every day, quite possibly the only ones they owned. And these were the lucky few that actually gained admission to a university, in a country where less than one percent of the populace was privileged to move on to higher study. Even if a student did manage to make it through college, he or she still faced the depressing prospect of working for woefully substandard wages in China's financially strapped educational system while their budding capitalist peers laughed all the way to the bank. Was it any wonder that demoralized Chinese students would rise up and demand fairness and an end to corruption at their first opportunity?

A day or two after Hu's death, I showed up at my English conversation class to find only a half-dozen of my 30 students at their desks. I waited a while for the no-shows before starting the day's lesson but soon noticed that all of the students were visibly distracted. It wasn't hard to see why, for hundreds of their peers were just then noisily passing below the second-story classroom windows on their way to join mourners massing beneath the gigantic statue of Chairman Mao in Chengdu's centrally located Tianfu Square. Several awkward minutes passed before a student named Knight stammered, "Mr. Dennis, please forgive us, but we must go and join our classmates." I understood fully and gave them my blessing to leave. Although a month or more still remained in the spring semester, it was to be my last class until autumn.

Long indifferent to politics, the mild-mannered chemists and polymer scientists of Chengdu University of Science and Technology had finally been goaded into action by political activists from nearby Sichuan University, who gathered outside the campus gates taunting our students with accusations of selfishness and cowardice. Across the road at Sichuan Music Conservatory, posters targeting the music students likewise aroused the latent democratic spirit in the bohemians. Scholars from Western Medical University soon followed suit, marching down Renmin ("People's") Road waving placards in their emergency-room whites.

An almost festive atmosphere prevailed as the ranks of protesters swelled in Tianfu Square. When Anne and I made a trip to the city center to see what was afoot, we found hundreds of young people encamped at the base of the towering Mao statue, now sporting dozens of homemade banners inscribed with inflammatory slogans. Student organizers led daily marches through the city center, bringing the already chaotic traffic to a standstill. Shopkeepers and office workers fortified the students with food and drink and shouted encouragement from upstairs windows. It seemed that all Chengdu supported the students' cause.

There was some suspicion among government officials that the demonstrations were not entirely spontaneous but had been engineered by a subterranean network of pro-democracy activists. While many dismissed this theory as typical government propaganda, I did feel that the apparent synchronicity of events among widely scattered cities argued in favor of a coordinated campaign. However, it was clear to me that the vast majority of student participants were motivated by nothing more than naïve idealism and patriotic zeal. If they were indeed being manipulated by shadowy forces, most were ignorant of the fact.

Intoxicated by their apparent success, students across China widened their demands over the next few weeks to include freedom of speech and of the press. By now the protesters were courting disaster with their provocative antigovernment statements, but few were old enough to remember the cautionary horrors of the Cultural Revolution. Every night demonstrators would march around our campus chanting pro-democracy slogans, singing "The Internationale," and massing in front of the faculty apartments to openly harangue the university president. I wondered how long this recklessly defiant behavior could continue before something snapped.

Yet as the weeks passed, the protests in Chengdu visibly lost momentum. By June 3 the downtown encampment had dwindled to about 20 die-hard picketers, led by a megaphone-wielding woman from Chengdu Normal University who railed on tirelessly in the shadow of Mao. When Anne and I strolled through the area that afternoon, we observed that the citizenry now seemed positively bored with the students' broadsides. No doubt things would soon return to normal.

June 4 dawned fair and humid, an unusually pleasant Sichuan summer's day that betrayed no hint of the tremors that were already rattling China. It was the day of the foreign teachers' annual field trip to the dragon-boat races in the small Yangtze River port city of Leshan. The expats at KeDa had all been looking forward to this break from academic routine and had stockpiled plenty of beer for the 10-hour bus ride.

Just minutes before we were to board the bus at 10 A.M., an American teacher who had been listening to the BBC World Service on her shortwave radio raced up to our apartment and blurted out news of the world-shaking massacre at Tiananmen Square. All of the foreign teachers had been following the events in Beijing as closely as possible—which basically meant reading the opposite into whatever the official media was reporting—but we were completely stunned at the ferocity of the government crackdown. Minutes later, reports arrived that fighting had also broken out right on our doorstep in Chengdu.

Amid all this confusion Liu Kai-Zhong, a timid career bureaucrat who worked in the university's office of international affairs, hurried to the Panda Palace in a panic and breathlessly informed us that the trip to Leshan was being canceled because of the crisis. Incredibly, some of the missionaries who sermonized at KeDa actually had the nerve to complain about their holiday being scuttled. Mr. Liu rushed off to receive further orders.

The anxious foreign teachers gathered to share news and decide what to do next. A few minutes later a haggard-looking Mr. Liu reappeared with one of his superiors and announced that the field trip would go on as planned. His spontaneous decision to cancel the excursion had evidently been a serious *faux pas*, for university administrators wanted nothing more than to get the foreigners out of town and fast. Although they claimed to be concerned for our welfare, Mr. Liu and his bosses clearly wanted to prevent us from witnessing the escalating conflict in Chengdu. The callous missionaries and many of the other foreign teachers and scholars filed passively onto the bus to enjoy their holiday in Leshan, oblivious to the crisis. The rest of us rejected Mr. Liu's repeated urgings and remained behind, determined not to let school functionaries shelter us from the momentous events unfolding around us.

Certain that we would never get the truth from university officials or the Chinese media, Anne and I decided to bicycle into the city at once and witness the melee firsthand. Accompanied by American filmmaker Kim Nygaard and Italian nutritionist Tommaso Cavalli-Sforza, we pedaled our clunky bikes across campus with a mounting sense of dread and soon encountered bands of confused and visibly shaken students hurrying back to their dormitories. At the university gate we got our first taste of the violence that awaited us downtown, as two dazed youths carried a wounded classmate home on their shoulders, his head wrapped in a sickening blood-crimsoned towel.

We soon overtook hundreds of young people hurrying into the city from the suburbs and outlying countryside. Many of the protesters were mere children, armed with stones, bottles, chisels, and other makeshift weapons. Anger and fear hung thick in the air, amplified by menacing explosions in the distance. Turning onto the city's main thoroughfare, Renmin Road, we gasped to see the distant Mao statue wrapped in a shroud of thick smoke.

The four of us pedaled warily down Renmin Road, merging with an ever-growing swarm of citizens converging on Mao's monument. The scene grew increasingly chaotic as we drew nearer to the crux of the conflict. Billows of tear gas drifted up the street to a soundtrack of thunderous detonations. Bands of people fled past us in a panic, many of them injured. Strangely, the police were nowhere to be seen.

At length we crossed the main bridge over the Jinjiang River and entered the thick of the tumult. At intervals the acrid smoke thinned enough to afford us glimpses of a desperate battle raging beneath the outstretched arms of Chairman Mao. Thousands of anxious onlookers clogged the streets; every few minutes an ear-shattering blast would send them stampeding backward in wide-eyed fright. The very atmosphere was charged with hostility.

I turned at the sound of an approaching vehicle and spotted a police motorcycle chugging into the fray bearing a uniformed officer in a sidecar. The driver foolishly piloted the motorcycle straight into the crowd and was instantly beset by a mob of enraged citizens. Realizing their folly, the two cops pulled a quick 180 and raced back to safety, all the while maintaining a stoic composure. It must have been a terrifying inversion of justice for officials long accustomed to absolute power.

We locked our bicycles to a railing and cautiously strode forward until we found our way blocked by a human chain about 100 yards from the vortex of the fighting, near a small hospital that was the closest medical facility to the scene. Here, ordinary citizens had joined hands to create a safe passageway for the dozens of wounded people being rushed into the hospital. We watched in horror as volunteers hauled a steady stream of bloodied victims into the clinic on stretchers, vendors' carts, bicycles, and other makeshift conveyances.

Before long an agitated doctor came out of the hospital and implored Kim to photograph some of the victims so that the world could witness the atrocities committed by the government. Kim and

Anne followed the doctor to a large room filled with severely injured men, women, and children, many with gruesome head wounds. Kim captured the grisly scene on camera and promised the doctor that she would make every effort to get the negatives out of the country; some of her photographs eventually did appear in Italian newspapers. We wondered what would befall the courageous doctors and nurses who were defying explicit government orders not to treat the wounded.

A few minutes later a carelessly disguised policeman tried to enter the hospital. The infuriated crowd sniffed him out at once and fell on him like a flock of buzzards, brutally stomping the life out of him right before our eyes. My mind reeled at this harsh dispensation of vigilante justice, which graphically underscored the depth of the people's antipathy toward the police.

Outside the hospital, the crowd swept us up as it surged and retreated in waves to the sound of shouting at the battlefront. Stung by tear gas and fearful of getting trampled, we threaded our way back through the angry multitudes to the Jinjiang Hotel, site of the U.S. Consulate and the preferred hangout of Chengdu's expatriates. We ascended to the hotel's rooftop restaurant in hopes of making an aerial reconnaissance but could see little in the dense pall. On our way back down, a German tourist brazenly lit up a cigarette in the elevator. A British woman quickly swung around and barked, "I beg your pardon—don't you know it's *rude* to smoke in the elevator?" The smoker exhaled a generous lungful in her direction and replied, "If you don't like this, you *really* won't like it out there on the street!" It was the one moment of comic relief in an otherwise harrowing week.

Back on the streets, we decided to circumnavigate Tianfu Square at a safe distance to get a different perspective on the day's grim spectacle. By this time the crowd had swelled to as many as 100,000 citizens in my estimation. We continued to encounter people with frightful wounds, including one poor old fruit vendor who'd had his head split open simply for parking his cart in the wrong place at the wrong time. Everywhere we went, protesters greeted us with loud cheers, grateful that a few foreign observers were putting themselves at risk to witness their struggle. The official media's claims that rioters were attacking foreigners were nonsense, for the demonstrators plainly viewed us as sympathizers. Not surprisingly, we were later informed that photographs taken of us that day by plainclothes officers were posted prominently in police headquarters.

Worn down by the sight of so much carnage, we bicycled back to the university at twilight to find hundreds of panicked students fleeing the campus with hastily packed suitcases and cheap nylon carryall bags. The terrified scholars scattered to the city's train and bus stations, where many were apprehended by waiting police; others were eventually tracked down in their hometowns and ordered back to Chengdu for prolonged interrogation. Once back at the Panda Palace, we learned that all but a handful of the foreign teachers had decided to bail out of the country the next day aboard hastily chartered flights. I was seriously tempted to follow suit and even packed my bags in preparation, but a cool-headed Anne persuaded me to wait out the crisis, arguing that our presence might in some small way mitigate the inevitable crackdown to come. Our students likewise urged us not to abandon them in the troubled times that surely lay ahead. In the end, I was glad we decided to stay behind; otherwise, I would never have been able to recount the events that followed.

Incredibly, that night a student showed up at my door and asked me to give him a guitar lesson. I could hardly believe his seeming indifference to the tragedy that was convulsing his city, but perhaps this was his way of shutting the horror out of his mind. (Years later, the same student wrote me in Seattle with a request to find him an American wife; I couldn't even bring myself to reply.)

Bit by bit we managed to piece together what had happened in the early hours of June 4. According to witnesses, well after midnight—just as the final assault on the Tiananmen demonstrators was getting underway in Beijing—police vehicles had raced into the city center and hauled away the handful of protesters still camped under the Mao statue. A few students slipped the net and raced back to their respective campuses to rouse their classmates, who had already been alerted to the violence in Tiananmen Square via BBC shortwave broadcasts. Around daybreak, thousands of students from the city's universities marched to the city center in protest, only to find the area secured by a large paramilitary force from the Public Security Bureau. The incensed students hurled taunts and shoes at the stone-faced police, a provocation that supposedly justified the ensuing violence.

A tense standoff continued until, at a seemingly predetermined moment, the police suddenly assailed the protesters with a fury. Scores of cops poured out of the civil defense tunnels hidden beneath the Mao monument (ironically, now a subterranean shopping mall) and spilled into the crowd, dealing out vicious blows with truncheons. A student friend who was near the front lines later described how the police had lashed out indiscriminately at men, women, and children alike. Rather than immobilize protesters with blows to the legs, as is common practice in riot control, the enforcers deliberately aimed at their victims' heads, hence the large number of serious head injuries we witnessed. Most of the stunned students ran for their lives as soon as the first wave of violence broke, but they were quickly replaced by hundreds of outraged workers and citizens, who set fire to government vehicles and heaved paving stones and other debris at the police.

In addition to heavy-duty metal truncheons, the police brandished high-pressure fire hoses, stun grenades, and electric cattle prods. A student of ours who had connections to a local cattle-prod manu-facturer later told us that the Public Security Bureau had placed an unusually large order some weeks before the June events, suggesting that the action had been carefully orchestrated. It also came out that the paramilitary squads included a contingent of ethnic minority police who had been transported long distances to Chengdu for the occasion. Since these imported mercenaries had no ties to the local people and little love for their Chinese overlords, they reportedly relished the opportunity to beat up on the protesters. At least the cops weren't using firearms, as far as we knew.

After an uneasy night punctuated by distant explosions, Anne and I awoke to wild rumors running rampant through Chengdu. The fighting had intensified after nightfall, drawing still more combatants and leaving areas of the city in flames. Initial estimates of casualties ran in the hundreds. A story was circulating that the megaphone-wielding student spokeswoman from Chengdu Normal University had been bayoneted and left on the steps of police headquarters to serve as a warning to the unruly masses. A foreigner had supposedly been injured in the fighting; the army was said to be massing outside the city; and a round-the-clock curfew was now in effect in the city center. Our campus was virtually deserted.

In the early afternoon we decided to risk going back into the city, together with American teachers Dennis and Liz Houghton, two of the few foreigners who chose to wait out the turbulence in Chengdu. An eerie calm had fallen on the city, whose normally bustling streets were nearly empty of vehicles and pedestrians. Taking advantage of this lull in the violence, we cautiously inched our way toward the Mao statue to survey the damage. All around us lay a spectacle of appalling destruction. Livid at the brutal police attack, citizens had smashed every street lamp, ripped sturdy iron fences right out of the pavement, and pried loose most of the paving stones to launch at their assailers. A dozen or more burned-out trucks, buses, and jeeps littered the roadways, some still in flames. A propaganda-inscribed banner that had long festooned Mao's pedestal was reduced to burnt tatters; I wished I had been present to witness the sight of the Great Helmsman scattering his benedictions atop a wall of flame. Protesters had shattered every pane of glass in the many government buildings fronting Dongfeng Road but had pointedly spared the private shops and residences just across the street. A nearby police station and cinema lay in smoldering ruins. Fire-blackened provincial government offices lined the debris-strewn boulevard, and a pile of charred bicycles at the roadside presented a strangely poignant image. Months later, one could still view the burned-out husks of buses that had been dragged out of sight behind the Mao statue.

A few blocks away, the People's Market was a smoking heap of ash and rubble, the target of a spectacular act of arson during the night's melee. The destruction of the market, which occupied an entire city block, became a key motif in the government's propaganda counter-attack, as official news organs blared on about the willful destruction of public property by the proverbial "handful of hooligans." Media spin-doctors were already hard at work trying to restore the government's damaged credibility, labeling the whole mess a "counterrevolutionary rebellion." Many citizens believed the government itself had set the market aflame to justify further use of force, pointing out that fire trucks didn't arrive until most of the complex was already consumed. A friend who worked in a city architect's office later revealed that the market had long since been slated for demolition anyway.

We assessed the devastation with a few other fascinated onlookers, sensing the ominous presence of the police behind the walls of a nearby government compound in which they had established their redoubt. The cops were surely recording our every move, but at this point we no longer cared about our reputations. Emboldened by the seeming calm, more curiosity seekers began advancing through the wreckage. All at once a deafening blast from a stun grenade ruptured the air and sent everyone running for cover. After the echoes died away, the oppressive silence returned, but we didn't trust the uneasy stillness and opted to head back to the university by a different route, now and then passing another burning vehicle.

That night explosions again shook the city as heavy fighting resumed. Officials had issued a general warning that anyone on the streets past a certain time would be forcibly removed by the paramilitary police, but huge crowds nevertheless turned out in defiance of the edict. By now, most of the combatants were ordinary working-class people and "waiting for work youth," a euphemism for China's legions of unemployed. It's doubtful that many of them had a clear idea of what they were fighting for. I'd wager that most of them weren't battling for high principles but rather to avenge the students and lash out at authority in general.

As a previously announced deadline passed, paramilitary forces began a sweep of the city center, driving the frantic crowd down Renmin Road toward the river. Many of the fleeing demonstrators sought refuge within the Jinjiang and Minshan hotels, hoping that the presence of foreigners and the U.S. Consulate would shield them from police violence, but they found the gates firmly barred against them. At the Jinjiang, the desperate crowd simply forced open the gates with a press of bodies. In the ensuing confusion, fires broke out and ground-floor windows burst in a cascade of shattered glass. Chinese authorities would later claim that this was an assault on the hotel that included incidents of looting, thus providing further justification for the display of brutality that soon followed.

Believing they were under attack, the terrified foreign hotel guests stampeded to the U.S. Consulate at the rear of the hotel. Consul General Jan de Wilde badly overreacted to the crisis, initially denying sanctuary to several foreign nationals. Worse yet, we were later informed by a Consulate insider that the flustered diplomat had not only alerted the U.S. Embassy that the Consulate was under attack, but also called on Chinese authorities for protection. Thus freed of all constraints, paramilitary forces stormed the hotel grounds and dealt mercilessly with the fleeing citizens. One anonymous witness whose room overlooked the hotel grounds described watching police viciously crushing prone citizens' skulls with truncheons. Kim Nygaard, who observed the fray from an upstairs hotel room, told of soldiers seizing people, binding them with wire with enough force to break bones, and heaving them into trucks; she was certain that most of the victims didn't survive. Other onlookers claimed that police summarily dispatched some victims with a bullet to the head.

The horrific battle of the Jinjiang Hotel proved to be the final gasp of the three-day struggle. After that, even the most defiant protesters quickly vanished into the scenery. People's Liberation Army troops took up position at strategic locations just outside the city, and an edgy peace descended on the city. Rumors of civil war in Beijing fueled a rush of panic buying as Chengdu residents formed long queues outside grocery shops to stock up on provisions for the uncertain times ahead. Among the first consumer items to vanish from store shelves were shortwave radios, the only means of obtaining unfiltered news of the events wracking China.

People reversed their ideological positions overnight. Even the most ardent advocates of democratic reform now conceded the "necessity" of their government's actions in the face of widespread social disorder. Crusaders who had hotly denounced Deng Xiaoping yesterday were true-red Communist Party sycophants today. Government propaganda outlets monotonously drummed forth fictionalized accounts of the week's events and made much of the alleged attack on the foreigners and the consulate. The fusillade of editorials and carefully manipulated footage so blurred reality that even eyewitnesses began to doubt their own experiences.

The number of casualties may never be accurately assessed. Government spokesmen predictably insisted that no deaths had occurred—later revising the death toll to three—and claimed that most of the wounded were heroic policemen who had been savagely attacked by "counterrevolutionaries." Unofficial casualty estimates varied widely between several dozen and several hundred killed. We knew for a fact that there had been deaths, because we had witnessed the killing of the policeman and because many of the severely wounded victims we had seen were unlikely to survive their injuries. Credible reports of casualties also came in from workers at various city hospitals. One police officer, the brother of a close friend, told us that numerous bodies had been dragged behind police barricades where the public couldn't see them—he thought 100 dead was a conservative estimate. Years later, a friend's father who had access to internal government documents said that the death toll now stood at more than 300. By the late 1990s, some experts even claimed that more lives were lost in Chengdu than in Beijing. Whatever the final tally, the world at large still knows little of the events in Chengdu, as the international press was fixated almost exclusively on the situation in the Chinese capital. It would be fully 25 years until a detailed account besides my own finally surfaced in the mainstream Western media, with the June 4, 2014 publication of U.S. National Public Radio reporter Louisa Lim's *The People's Republic of Amnesia: Tiananmen Revisited*, which includes a chapter on the Chengdu events.

In the tense months following the June conflagration, party officials summoned student demonstrators back to Chengdu and interrogated them repeatedly about their involvement in the disturbances. Police grilled one of my guitar students at length about a sightseeing trip he'd made to Beijing in the spring, convinced that he'd gone there to hatch plots with counterrevolutionary rebels. A noticeable pall fell over the city, but the crackdown in Chengdu was never as severe as anticipated, certainly nothing like the witch-hunt carried out in Beijing. Remembering the outpouring of goodwill that had marked the first days of the student demonstrations, I could only surmise that many local government officials secretly sympathized with the students and rebellious citizens. After all, the Sichuanese did enjoy a long tradition of defying imperial authority.

A month after order was restored, university officials informed us that all the remaining foreign teachers in Chengdu were to be honored at a banquet hosted by provincial government leaders. The banquet was ostensibly a gesture of thanks to the "foreign friends" who contributed to China's educational and economic development. Unfortunately for the politicos, the mayhem in June had reduced the province's contingent of 200 foreign residents to about 10 hardy souls. Afraid of losing face, officials at our school stressed that our attendance was mandatory. Anne boldly opted to skip the event, sensing some kind of setup, a decision that temporarily landed her in the doghouse with university administrators.

The KeDa contingent was taken to a reception room in the Jinjiang Hotel, where we joined the half-dozen other foreigners still living in Chengdu. I noted with alarm that a TV crew had set up several cameras in the room. A few minutes later our hosts ushered in the provincial dignitaries and we all settled into maroon velvet sofas draped with lace antimacassars. The cameras started whirring, and after a round of introductions the provincial governor, Hang Banyan, stepped up to the podium. Speaking through an interpreter, Hang gave us the government's version of the June events: The turmoil was the work of the storied "handful" of counterrevolutionaries; the antigovernment demonstrations had been incited by hostile foreign powers; the only casualties of the fighting were defenseless police officers; and on and on. He then spoke a few words in Chinese while the TV cameras slowly panned across the foreign teachers.

After the speech, our hosts brought us to a banquet room and seated us at circular dining tables. Embarrassed by Anne's absence, a nervous official instructed me to sit in her designated place—right next to the provincial governor. The organizers had bestowed this honor on Anne because of her seniority among the remaining teachers and her fluency in Chinese. As the dinner courses came and went, I carefully navigated my way through a conversation with the governor, who spoke English reasonably well. To my surprise, he asked me what I thought of the June events—here was my opportunity to give a high government official an earful about the regime's appalling treatment of its citizens! But as I hoped to remain in China a while longer, I deemed it more prudent to withhold comment. Later in the meal, the governor struck me speechless by commenting that I looked like Michael Jackson.

Several weeks after the banquet I ran into a student who remarked that he'd seen me on TV. "But don't worry," he assured me, "we don't believe the things they said about you." When I pressed him for more information, he explained that the teachers at the banquet had been singled out as the "brave foreign friends who stayed through the counterrevolutionary rebellion to show their support for the government's policies." To my lasting embarrassment, the clip was aired again and again over the next few months.

Toward the end of the year, consular officials invited Anne and me to a reception for the U.S. Ambassador to China, James Lilley, a quintessential Cold War ideologue who seemed mildly amused at my exploits as an American musician in the Chinese hinterlands. Lilley went on to give the assembled guests the official U.S. view of the June events and their aftermath, confidently concluding that "we" were winning the battle for the hearts and minds of the Chinese people. A quarter-century later, in the wake of a series of damaging Bush-era military misadventures that further eroded U.S. relations with an increasingly powerful and self-confident China, Lilley's smug certitude has proven to be ludicrously off the mark.

# CHAPTER 7

# THE BANANA PANCAKE TRAIL

In the aftermath of the June 4 upheaval, I took advantage of the long break in my teaching schedule to travel throughout western China, visiting scenic, cultural, and historical sites and gaining exposure to musical traditions that would strongly influence the way I listen to and create music. I also welcomed the opportunity to take my mind off the brutal events of the previous month.

My first excursion was a two-week solo trip to southwestern China's Yunnan Province. Described in typically romantic fashion in Chinese tourist brochures as the "Land South of the Clouds," Yunnan is an age-old cultural crossroads linking East, Central, and South Asia and is home to more than two dozen ethnic minority peoples, including the Yi, Wa, Naxi, Yao, Dai, and Pumi nationalities. Most of the province occupies a high, pleasantly balmy plateau, fringed by tropical rainforest in the south and the imposing corrugated mountain ranges of the Tibetan borderlands to the northwest.

After a southbound overnight rail journey on the many-tunneled Chengdu-Kunming line, hacked through unforgiving mountain ribs at the cost of hundreds of conscripted laborers' lives, I disembarked near the belching smokestacks of the massive Panzhihua Iron Works and boarded a bus to the small city of Lijiang near the Burmese border. For the better part of the day the groaning, battered vehicle inched its way up a series of dizzying switchbacks in ever more elevated terrain, rolling wearily into Lijiang in the early evening. Grateful to escape the cramped confines of the bus, I made my way on foot through the narrow lanes of the Old Town to the modest guesthouse that was the default lodging for foreign travelers, pausing now and then to admire the tiled roofs and whitewashed walls of traditional Lijiang dwellings.

Lijiang is the cultural seat of the Naxi people, a small ethnic group that shares many characteristics with the neighboring Tibetans. The Naxi have long exerted a fascination on Western ethnologists on account of their shamanistic, matrilineal society and unique pictographic script, traditions that still survive precariously in spite of the best efforts of Red Guards to stamp out Naxi beliefs in the 1960s and 70s.

The highlight of my stay in Lijiang was an outdoor concert by the elderly Dayan Ancient Music Association, among the last remaining purveyors of a venerable Taoist musical tradition tempered by Buddhist and Confucian influences. Performed by a small orchestra of Naxi octogenarians, the Dongjing ritual music—slow, courtly unison melodies punctuated by eerie gong and cymbal passages—palpably conveyed the distant strains of a vanished era. It's a small miracle that this musical anachronism and its orally transmitted repertoire survived the upheavals of the twentieth century.

After the concert I visited with Naxi ethnomusicologist Xuan Ke, the association's indefatigable director and something of a local character. As we sipped tea in the study of his traditional timbered house, Xuan Ke wistfully lamented what he felt was the inevitable disappearance of the orchestra and its repertoire. A few of the superannuated musicians were already on their last legs, and younger Naxi people, seduced by the ways of the modern world, showed little interest in carrying on their elders' tradition. Fearing the extinction of an irreplaceable musical legacy, foreign music scholars had been perennially frustrated in their efforts to document the Naxi music by Chinese officials, who saw little merit in preserving this "backward" art form. Fortunately, the Dayan Ancient Music Association enjoyed a revival a few years after my visit with the recruitment of several new members, including the first woman to learn the repertoire. The group has since performed abroad to great acclaim, and high-quality recordings of their music are now widely available outside China. Listening to my own amateur tape of the Dayan musicians never fails to evoke the haunting stillness of a warm Yunnan summer's evening.

Xuan Ke's life story is an apt metaphor for China's turbulent modern history. When Communist forces wrested Yunnan's capital city of Kunming from Nationalist control in 1949, Xuan Ke, a devotee of Western classical music, welcomed the victorious troops to town by conducting the local orchestra in a performance of Schubert's "March Militaire." Far from earning him the gratitude of the new regime, Xuan Ke's passion for Western music instead landed him in prison for a total of 21 years, including seven months in lightless solitary confinement. He claims that the only thing that saved him from going blind or insane during his incarceration was his obsessive chanting of a Naxi healing song. Xuan Ke's horrendous stint in captivity gave him a new appreciation for his Naxi musical heritage, and when he was finally set free, he devoted his remaining days to preserving the ancient Dongjing repertoire through his patronage of the Naxi Orchestra. At the time of my visit, Xuan Ke was still considered a bad element by local Chinese officials, who frowned on his contacts with foreign researchers and music lovers.

Yuan Yuhai was Naxi musician of an altogether different sort. An attractive middle-aged woman who ran a pleasant little restaurant that I frequented during my stay in Lijiang, Yuan recruited me to help her buy a guitar for the use of her patrons. I accompanied her to a government department store and selected the least flawed of several sad-looking instruments on display, a badly warped acoustic model that cost her about US$15. That night after dinner, I tried my best to entertain the disinterested foreign diners at Yuan's behest, nearly spraining my fingers on the cable-strength guitar strings. Afterward, Yuan brought out a book filled with hundreds of traditional folk songs of the Naxi, Dai, Hani, Sani, Yi, Tibetan, and other Yunnan peoples. For the rest of the evening she sang dozens of tunes in an evocative, keening voice, to the apparent dismay of regular customers, who had doubtless heard the routine before. For my part, I was deeply impressed by her ability to remember all these melodies and sing in so many different languages. Yuan later explained that as a younger woman, she had won honors for her folk singing and had traveled throughout China performing ethnic music for the masses. She had even given a concert in faraway Beijing, an event she recalled with shining eyes.

Yuan's restaurant catered to the tastes of foreign travelers who steadily passed through Lijiang on the so-called Banana Pancake Trail. Connecting such Asian hippie shrines as Dali and Xishuangbanna in southwest China, Kashgar and Turfan on the Silk Road, Kuta Beach in Bali, Pattaya in Thailand, and Goa in India, the trail was then heavily traveled by thousands of young Europeans and Americans, some bent on experiencing the mythical "real" Asia, others pursuing their notion of an Eastern spiritual quest. United in their antipathy toward the Han Chinese majority, these wayfarers studiously avoided straying into the Chinese cultural heartland whenever possible. You could always tell which direction the Banana Pancake trekkers were traveling by the clothes they wore—embroidered Uighur caps from Turkistan and brightly colored scarves from Tibet marked those coming from the north, while loose-fitting blue batik outfits made in Dali were *de rigeur* for those arriving from the south. All along the route, locals capitalized on the trekker traffic by opening inexpensive bunkhouses and vegan restaurants with names like the Coca-Cola Café, which offered such hipster fare as banana pancakes—hence the circuit's name. Some of these places even sold pot if you knew how to ask. (I was surprised to learn that cannabis products were widely available in China, though the Chinese themselves largely eschewed their use, which was mostly confined to the Muslim and expatriate communities.)

Fifty kilometers north of Lijiang, the snowmelt-swollen Yangtze River plunges down from the heights of the Tibetan Plateau and corkscrews through the celebrated Tiger-Leaping Gorge. At 3,000 meters deep, Hutiaoxia, as it is known in Chinese, is one of the most awe-inspiring ravines on the planet. Bracketed by soaring precipices in the shadow of 5,500-meter Jade Dragon Snow Mountain, the gorge is so constricted at its narrowest point that a tiger under pursuit by hunters is said to have vaulted from one side to the other. A narrow footpath chiseled into the face of the gorge's northern escarpment gives precarious passage above the Yangtze's boulder-strewn flume, a violently foaming cauldron that has claimed the lives of more than one foolhardy whitewater adventurer. I was keen to hike this storied path through the Tiger-Leaping Gorge and found a willing partner in Michael, a white Kenyan who shared my cheap traveler's dormitory in Lijiang.

The normal approach to Hutiaoxia was to take a bus to the town of Qiaotou on the river's far bank and then follow the cliffside track to the chasm's downstream outlet, a trek of roughly two days' duration. Here travelers could pay a boatman to ferry them back across the river to the humble village of Daju, from which there was infrequent bus service back to Lijiang.

This year, however, Chinese authorities had temporarily closed all Tibetan cultural areas because of recent unrest in Tibet. The proscribed area included the entire north bank of the Tiger-Leaping Gorge, which lay in a so-called autonomous Tibetan prefecture. Foreign travelers were now being turned back at the Qiaotou bridge under threat of heavy fines or deportation, so the only feasible approach to the gorge was a little-used dirt road over the mountains to the hamlet of Daju on the still-accessible south bank. As luck would have it, Michael and I had just missed the weekly bus to Daju, so we decided to take our chances hitchhiking instead. According to the guidebook *Southwest China Off the Beaten Track*, thumbing a ride was a viable option because the road saw a fair amount of logging-truck traffic.

Michael and I set out in high spirits on a postcard-perfect summer morning, expecting to reach Daju by early afternoon and then cross the Yangtze and hike deep into the gorge to the rustic guesthouse where we planned to spend the night. Since we planned to sleep under a roof, we traveled light and took little more than an extra layer of clothing. We would purchase food along the way if necessary.

After a spell of unproductive hitchhiking at the edge of town, we started down the road on foot and walked about six kilometers on the sun-scorched pavement before the driver of a flatbed truck finally offered us a lift. As the truck drew away from Lijiang, cultivated fields soon gave way to pleasant coniferous woodland and subalpine meadows as we ascended a flank of lofty Jade Dragon Snow Mountain in the sharp high-country air. My companion and I sat in the open truck bed and soaked in the vista, certain that we would soon reach our destination. Five minutes later the driver abruptly deposited us at a lonely road junction in the forest about 20 kilometers outside Lijiang, less than a quarter of the distance to Daju. We waited here for northbound traffic until we grew bored and then started walking again to pass the time. At least the scenery was splendid; after spending months in brutally deforested regions of China, I savored the sight and scent of healthy trees.

We walked several kilometers toward Daju in the growing midday heat, traversing the mountain's densely wooded lower slopes. No traffic passed our way and, remarkably for populous China, we saw very few signs of human habitation. Shortly after noon we rounded a bend in the road and came upon a tiny agricultural settlement of the Yi people, a sizable ethnic group native to China's mountainous southwest. The morning's stiff walk had left us famished, as we had long since devoured the two packages of dry cookies that constituted our meager supplies. We hailed a villager and mimed eating gestures, hoping to appease our growling bellies. The man smiled in recognition and led us to a rough-hewn barn-like structure that functioned as the village commissary. No menu was necessary, for the only dish available in this impoverished hamlet was simple egg fried rice. In our road-worn condition, the plain fare tasted like a high-class spread, and we gratefully wolfed down our portions with gusto. Ignoring the protestations of our generous host, we left some money on the table to pay for the food and got back on the road. Surely some traffic would soon pass our way.

For hours we tramped northward along the dusty road without encountering a single vehicle. Footsore and cranky with fatigue, we loudly cursed the authors of our guidebook as we continued trudging forward, no longer paying heed to the glorious mountain landscapes. Late in the afternoon we finally heard the sound of an approaching motor vehicle. The two of us quickly stationed ourselves at the roadside and thrust out our thumbs as a large truck came into view—and sped on by without pausing. We muttered foul imprecations and resumed plodding ahead, passing the hours swapping life stories and daydreaming about the cool beers we would soon be guzzling in Daju.

At length we heard the unmistakable rumble of another truck gaining on us. Determined not to let this one get away, Michael brazenly stood in the middle of the road with arms outstretched, blocking the truck's passage. The driver skidded to a halt in a cloud of hot dust. Michael yelled "Daju!" and before the mystified driver could respond, we leaped into the back of the truck and wedged ourselves in among sacks of grain. The driver stepped down from the cab and unleashed a volley of invective. We just grinned like foreign idiots and intoned the word "Daju" repeatedly.

Moments later another truck pulled up behind us, only the fourth vehicle we'd seen all day. The two drivers conferred for a moment and then thoughtfully suggested that we ride in the roomier second truck. At last, a ride to Daju! But no sooner did Michael and I hop back down onto the road than both drivers promptly gunned their engines and vanished in a trail of grit, drowning out our howls of exasperation.

Thoroughly dispirited, we traipsed for miles and miles and more miles, at times tiptoeing past rustic Yi farmsteads guarded by snarling, half-feral dogs. The sun was already sinking behind Jade Dragon Snow Mountain to the west. By this time we had grudgingly accepted that we would have to spend the night in Daju and postpone our Tiger-Leaping Gorge hike until the following morning. Michael and I were now ravenous from our lengthy march. Our worsening fatigue was even starting to affect our judgment; now and then one of us would swear that he heard a truck in the distance, and we would both stand silent for long minutes straining our ears for a vehicle that never arrived. Indeed, we never saw another truck that day. I was in no mood to appreciate the ironic fact that I had often craved privacy in overcrowded China.

Toward dusk we chanced upon a timber camp where a logging crew was completing its day's work. Without ceremony we walked up and offered the loggers the considerable sum of 10 RMB to drive us the rest of the way to Daju in their *tuolaji*, an ungainly contraption that looked like a cross between a tractor and a small dinosaur. The bemused woodsmen waved us off like flies. Michael and I hobbled off cussing under our breath.

Night fell. We were now on the downhill portion of our journey, having crested a pass a few miles back. Daju surely couldn't be far now; we could even descry the village lights like glittering pinpricks down below. The tantalizing sight of human habitation gave us a fresh burst of enthusiasm, but our abused bodies rebelled. By now our feet screamed at every step. We were both wearing flimsy tennis shoes that were laughably inadequate for a long-distance trek. My calf muscles felt like jerked beef. So far I had refrained from griping about my aches and blisters, impressed by Michael's stoicism in the face of pain, but at this point even the physically robust Kenyan was showing the strain. We paused more and more frequently by the roadside, each time finding it harder to get back on our feet.

The road zigzagged with maddening repetition down the steep mountainside toward the Yangtze. Hours later, the lights of Daju seemed no closer than before. We had long since resigned ourselves to walking the rest of the way when we heard the welcome thrum of an engine behind us. Presently the loggers' *tuolaji* came into sight, bearing a cargo of freshly felled pines.

In desperation, we again blocked the road, forcing the flummoxed driver to slam on his brakes. Before he could react, we quickly scrambled up onto the stack of gnarled tree trunks roped to his cargo bed and announced that we were bound for Daju. The furious lumberman railed at us, demanding that we get the hell off his *tuolaji*. We instantly offered him 10, then 20 RMB, but he still refused to budge. After a brief standoff we obediently climbed back down onto the road. Before limping off toward Daju, I turned to the man and weakly said *"xie xie"*—thank you. My pathetic utterance evidently struck a chord of human sympathy in the lumberman, for he suddenly relented and gestured us back aboard with a grunt. We perched like rodeo riders atop the splintered logs as the *tuolaji* noisily bucked its way down the rutted dirt road.

Our bumpy ride in the rattletrap *tuolaji* felt like a cruise in a stretch limo after the day's travails, but it still didn't get us to Daju. After a mere five kilometers, the taciturn lumberman offloaded us at a place where a footpath crossed the road, signaling that it was a shortcut to town. We thanked him and watched regretfully as he sputtered off into the night, glad to be rid of the troublesome foreign devils.

We left the road and lowered ourselves mechanically down the trail, each step a world of agony. Hours had passed and still the lights of Daju appeared to be in a distant galaxy. At one point Michael simply sat down in a field and announced that he was going to sleep right on the spot. With thunderclaps now pealing threateningly in the distance, I didn't think snoozing in the open was a wise idea, so I helped my grumbling companion back to his feet and nudged him down the path. Right on cue, a prodigious thunderstorm broke moments later and drenched us to the skin.

Numb with soreness and exhaustion, we at last stumbled out onto the alluvial floodplain surrounding Daju. Here the path disappeared in a muddy fen, leaving us to slog through deep muck toward the now-darkened settlement. As we drew near the village, dozens of agitated dogs started howling in chorus. Delirious, sopping wet, and smeared to our knees with mire, we made our way to the only lighted house and banged on its closed gate. We soon heard the sound of approaching footsteps, and a small peephole in the door slid open to reveal a pair of wary eyes. A man gruffly asked what our business was. We trained flashlights on our faces to identify ourselves and replied that we were looking for the village guesthouse. The villager abruptly slammed the peephole shut and silently returned to his house.

We had begun to despair of finding shelter when a man hailed us from a nearby house and pointed out the guesthouse a few doors down the lane. Michael and I dragged ourselves the last few steps to the modest inn and roused the proprietor, a pleasant Naxi woman who didn't seem at all fazed by the sight of two drenched foreigners materializing out of the stormy night. Yes, a room was available. Equally important, she had a single precious bottle of warm local beer. Hallelujah!

Once inside our Spartan room, Michael and I gave each other great bear hugs, laughing wildly at our deliverance and swigging the stale beer like it was Dom Perignon. We had made it! It was well after 2 A.M., and we had just walked 75 kilometers—nearly 50 miles!—over the mountains in a single day, fueled by nothing more than a handful of cookies, a bowl of Yi egg fried rice, and a few mouthfuls of water. Strangers just two days earlier, the two of us were now bonded by our shared ordeal.

A sharp knock on the door interrupted our celebration. Thinking it was the Naxi innkeeper, I was startled to open the door on a frowning British woman who sneered, "Do you mind? People are trying to get some sleep around here!" (She must have arrived on the bus we'd missed the previous day.) Even here in remote Daju, after all that Michael and I had been through on this arduous day, we still couldn't shake the Banana Pancake Trailers. Completely drained, we fell heavily into our beds and slept like corpses.

We awoke in mid-afternoon with legs and feet so sore that we could barely walk across the room, let alone test our mettle against the rugged Tiger-Leaping Gorge. It quickly became apparent that we had no choice but to spend the day convalescing in Daju. But as we hadn't eaten a morsel since our paltry repast at the Yi village more than a day earlier, we reluctantly forced our rebellious limbs into motion and went out in search of a meal. The harsh glare of daylight revealed Daju to be a wretched, dirt-poor dump of a burg complete with hogs wallowing in muddy craters on the main drag. We limped shakily to the town's lone restaurant and woke the groggy cook from his afternoon slumber. The man rose, yanked a slab of grayish meat off a hook screwed into the ceiling, and then lifted the cover of the restaurant's single wok, disturbing dozens of angrily buzzing flies that made their home inside it. Our appetites instantly dulled, we chose to forgo this delicacy and stumbled back to the hotel, where we managed to scare up steaming bowls of the ubiquitous egg fried rice. Back in our room, we medicated ourselves with more watery beer before descending into comatose slumber.

The next day we rose bright and early, still stiff as cadavers but determined to hike the fabled gorge if it killed us. Our next challenge would be to persuade the notoriously ornery boatman to ferry us to the other side of the Yangtze, where we would pick up the trail that led through the gorge. According to travelers we had met in Lijiang, the ferryman would take foreigners across for 10 RMB, a mere US$1.50 but still considered a rip-off by the skinflint Westerners who'd admonished us not to spoil things for everyone else by giving the poor boatman too much cash.

My companion and I hobbled out of town to a bluff overlooking the Yangtze, from which we espied the ferryman's boat tied up on the far shore. The pilot himself was nowhere to be seen. Examining the near bank, we made out what looked like a boat slip some distance downstream and decided to wait for the ferryman there. We made our way painfully down a footpath to the water's edge. Just as we reached the riverbank, a man hailed us from atop the bluff we'd just descended and indicated that the ferry slip was actually a few hundred meters upstream from where we stood. Loath to climb all the way back up the trail, we opted to make a lateral shortcut across the face of the bluff until we found a convenient place to drop down to the landing. Like many such undertakings, it looked a lot easier than it really was. The slope was highly unstable soil and clay, with only clumps of loose dirt and fragile weeds to serve as handholds. A slip would mean certain death in the churning waters barreling out of the gorge. My legs trembled like a seismograph. For one gut-wrenching moment the ground gave way beneath my feet, leaving me clinging to a slender root for dear life. But the Yangtze didn't claim me this time, and we eventually made our way safely down to the ferry dock.

We sat at the water's edge and waited for the ferryman. The sun climbed slowly into the sky, burning off the clammy morning mist. As the hours wore on without any sign of our transport, we realized with dismay that we might have to spend yet another night in cheer-less Daju. Eventually we both dozed off, lulled to drowsiness by the dull roar of the Yangtze issuing from the gorge upstream. Around midday we awoke to the sound of voices and caught sight of three young Tibetan women descending to the landing en route to their village on the far side of the river. We bantered with the friendly Tibetans to pass the time, eliciting gales of laughter with our falter-ing Chinese. A few moments later we noticed movement on the opposite bank and saw the elusive boatman boarding his vessel. It dawned on us that he had almost certainly seen us hours earlier but would only bother to cross the river for locals.

The skipper skillfully maneuvered his weathered rowboat across the swift brown current, nosed in at the near shore, and gestured the Tibetan women aboard. Before Michael and I could follow suit, he pushed off from the bank with his pole, glowering at us fiercely. We at once leapt into the departing craft, barely managing to get aboard without a dunking. The apoplectic boatman whirled around in his seat and ordered us off his boat. We stood firm, determined not to be turned back this close to our destination after all the grief we'd been through. Michael reached into his pocket and thrust a 10 RMB note at the raging ferryman, who refused the bribe with a fresh volley of abuse. An additional 10 RMB did the trick. Pocketing his 20 big ones, the skipper aimed his prow at the far bank and rowed us across, cursing the whole way. We had no doubt messed things up for all future cheapskate travelers by doubling the stakes, but in our condition we really didn't give a damn.

Once disembarked on the far bank, we hurried upriver into the narrowing Tiger-Leaping Gorge with all the speed our beat-up legs could muster. We had finally reached our elusive destination, fully two days later than anticipated. As the ancient footpath angled steadily upward across the canyon's steepening north wall, fearsome precipices on both sides of the river drew closer together, framing a slender stripe of pale sky two vertical miles above. A few hundred feet below the trail the Yangtze tore through its granite defile with the pressure of a fire hose, sending up a frightful din that muffled all other sounds and rendered conversation futile. I marveled at the primordial, almost oppressive grandeur of this rude gash in the face of the earth, but it was difficult to fully savor the spectacle when every blistered footstep felt like firewalking. We nevertheless managed to make decent progress in our gingerly fashion and estimated that we would reach the Walnut Grove guesthouse before nightfall. In the late afternoon we passed a pleasant cabin with an amazing view of the gorge and regretted that we would not be spending the night there. According to the directions and timing given in *Southwest China Off the Beaten Path,* the Walnut Grove guesthouse still lay some miles ahead.

The cliffside track threaded through avalanche scars and skirted dramatic waterfalls as it hugged the escarpment above the white-capped torrent. Now and then the landscape opened out into subalpine pastures dotted with grazing sheep and the occasional Tibetan herdsman. In one such clearing we found a tiny cluster of buildings, one of which was surely the guesthouse. But when we asked a

Tibetan villager for directions to our lodgings, he broke out in hearty laughter and informed us that Walnut Grove lay several hours' journey back in the direction from which we'd come. Our guidebook's vague directions had bedeviled us yet again—we had walked right past the guesthouse earlier in the day, convinced that Walnut Grove was miles away. In broken Chinese, we asked the local Tibetans if we could stay in their village, but they wanted nothing to do with us. In all fairness, we *were* trekking through an area that had been closed to foreign travelers by the Chinese government, so our presence in the village could have brought trouble to the Tibetans. Unsure what to do next, we bought bottles of tepid beer from the village trading post and sat on a rock at the edge of the village, giving our cracked feet a rest.

Obviously we couldn't hike all those miles back to Walnut Grove. Night was already gathering, and worse still, it had started raining heavily. I again regretted my shortsighted decision to leave my state-of-the-art camping gear back in Chengdu, fearing that this night could turn out to be even more miserable than our marathon stumble to Daju. We despaired of finding shelter in this vertiginous landscape, but then remembered the many caves we'd seen among jumbles of house-sized boulders during the day's trek. Perhaps there were more nearby? Hoisting our daypacks, we set off down the path and, to our immense relief, found a cave a few hundred meters from the village. What's more, it was dry and roomy enough to stand up in. Evidently we weren't the first creatures to shelter here, for the cave floor was carpeted with dried sheep dung. We kicked the sheep pies outside, disturbing a host of large, termite-like beetles that burrowed up through the sandy cave floor and scattered into the shadows, a sight hardly conducive to sleep.

Having foolishly left our sleeping bags in Lijiang, we hurriedly gathered armloads of tall weeds and fashioned makeshift mattresses on the cave floor. Our shelter now reasonably habitable, we ran back to the village in the pelting rain and bought as much beer and snack food as we could carry. As I sat by our small fire roasting slices of *wucanrou*—the Chinese version of Spam—I flashed back to the time when, as a small boy, I had fantasized about living in a cave. Here among the sheep shit and beetles, the reality wasn't nearly as romantic as I'd imagined, though in context the hot Spam, garnished with powder from a Ramen noodle flavor packet, was one of the finest meals of my life.

At dawn we awoke, chilled and disheveled, to find that the rain had intensified overnight, obscuring the far side of the canyon. Since the prospect of another night in our cave was hardly appealing, we hit the trail early and were almost instantly drenched from head to toe. Bedraggled and in a thoroughly foul humor, we hiked the remaining 10 or so kilometers out to the small town of Qiaotou at the head of the gorge, passing a gang of convict laborers hacking out the beginnings of an automobile road through the canyon.

Qiaotou was similarly off-limits to foreigners due to its location in the Tibetan prefecture, but by now we were far too wet and hungry to bother being evasive—the police could go ahead and deport us for all we cared. We boldly strode down the puddled main street and entered the first restaurant we saw. Big bowls of noodle soup and slices of translucent "thousand-year eggs" improved our disposition immeasurably. Suitably revived, we were just getting back to worrying about the police when a bus marked "Lijiang" pulled up right in front of the restaurant. What luck! We hopped aboard and made it back to Lijiang without incident, ducking our heads below the windows as we crossed the guarded bridge back over the Yangtze. Our trip to Tiger-Leaping Gorge, undertaken so casually, had turned into one of the stiffest ordeals of our lives. Regrettably, I never saw my excellent fellow traveler Michael again.

A week later I spent a night in a travelers' hostel in the provincial capital of Kunming, some 300 kilometers southeast of Lijiang. Comparing road stories with another foreign traveler, I mentioned that I'd just hiked through the Tiger-Leaping Gorge. The traveler replied that he'd recently heard about two crazy bastards who actually *walked* all the way from Lijiang to Tiger-Leaping Gorge in a day. Six months later I heard our story repeated by a Westerner passing through Chengdu. In such a way legends are born...

Despite all the hardship and frustration, I feel privileged to have made the trek to the Tiger-Leaping Gorge in the way that I did. Although Michael and I couldn't have known it at the time, ours was an experience that future visitors would never be able to repeat, for a two-lane highway now penetrates the gorge from end to end and tour buses disgorge hundreds of sightseers daily. Visitors now have to pay an admission fee to enter the gorge, currently disfigured by a half-dozen new guesthouses. The crusty old ferryman now does the bidding of the China Travel Service, and air-conditioned mini-buses ply the 90 long, hard kilometers from Lijiang to Daju every day of the week. Worse yet, at the time of this writing, the Chinese government is pushing ahead with plans to dam the river just below the gorge, an act of reckless hubris that would inundate one of the world's most astonishing and irreplaceable natural marvels.

# CHAPTER 8

# PANDASONIC

In August, while our students were undergoing compulsory "political reeducation" for taking part in the pro-democracy demonstrations, Anne and I traced the route of the storied Silk Road into China's far northwest. Joining us for the first part of the journey were Dennis and Liz Houghton, two American teachers we'd befriended in Chengdu.

A tortuous train journey through the furrowed highlands of Shaanxi and Gansu Provinces brought us to the dusty Yellow River port city of Lanzhou, where our teaching credentials secured us accommodations in the university guesthouse. Situated at the boundary of China proper and the Central Asian interior, Lanzhou exhibits a pronounced Islamic influence and is home to a large population of ethnic Chinese Muslims known as the Hui people. Our brief stopover in this drab city was notable chiefly for our first taste of Central Asian cuisine—fragrant rice pilaf, steaming discs of flatbread, lamb skewers dusted with chili and cumin—and for the startling sight of robust cannabis plants springing up through sidewalk cracks right in the heart of city.

Before striking out westward on the Silk Road, we made a three-day side trip to Qinghai Province to visit Ta'ersi, one of the most sacred lamaseries of Tibetan Buddhism. It was here on Tibet's northeastern frontier that the revered saint Tsong Kapa, founder of the dominant Yellow Hat sect, was born in 1357. Cupped by lofty hills resembling the frozen waves of a grassy sea, the walled lamasery compound contained several ornately decorated temples as well as smaller shrines, monks' living quarters, and a pleasant, brightly painted guesthouse, where we lodged for a mere pittance. Among the more celebrated features of Ta'ersi was an elaborate tableau of Buddhist saints sculpted entirely from pungent yak butter. The August heat had overcome the fetid saints, melting their limbs into grotesquely elongated, waxen cataracts. One Buddha in particular served as a poignant metaphor of mortal decay, his fallen head dissolving into an oleaginous mandala on the floor of the shrine.

Music was central to lamasery life. Each morning at dawn the air was rent by pneumatic blasts from 10-foot-long brass *dung* trumpets, and at intervals throughout the day scores of monks would assemble to intone scripture to the accompaniment of bells and gongs. (During our visit, the ritual music was all but drowned out by strident Chinese government propaganda spewing from loudspeakers positioned right outside the lamasery gate.) At a market stall outside the lamasery I purchased some crudely recorded cassettes of Qinghai folk music, a strangely affecting blend of pinched, reedy singing and cheap electric keyboards that evoked the lonesome, windswept steppes.

Leaving Ta'ersi, we doubled back to Lanzhou and boarded a train bound for the heart of the region historically known as Turkistan. Gazing out the train windows as we sped westward for 400 miles along the Silk Road, we were struck by the sight of cultivated hemp fields stretching for mile after mile, grown for fiber by the region's Muslim majority (not to mention other uses, as evidenced by the ubiquitous hashish sellers hawking their wares to tourists in the region's towns). At sundown we disembarked at the dusty frontier outpost of Jiayuguan at the western extremity of the Great Wall, at this point little more than an unimposing mud-brick barrier riddled with perforations. From here we traveled on by bus to the Gobi Desert oasis of Dunhuang, a journey prolonged by a three-hour engine breakdown in one of the least hospitable landscapes on the planet—a flat, featureless expanse resembling nothing more than an endless gravel-strewn parking lot. Back underway after makeshift repairs, we espied a dark smudge on the horizon that marked the verdant Dunhuang oasis, an island of green watered by snowmelt from the stark Qilian Mountains that form the northern wall of Tibet. Up close, the oasis vegetation turned out to be mostly hemp, which might explain the peculiar drowsiness that enveloped us for the length of our stay in the town. The next day we squeezed ourselves into a bus stuffed with Chinese and Japanese tourists to go admire the celebrated Buddhist frescoes of the honeycombed Mogao grottoes, preserved for more than a millennium by the arid atmosphere of the Gobi, though sadly diminished by plundering Western adventurers such as the infamous British archaeologist Sir Aurel Stein during the "golden age" of exploration. (A large part of Dunhuang's pilfered treasures currently resides in the British Museum, a source of continuing friction between the Chinese and UK governments.)

From Dunhuang, Dennis and Liz struck out on their own in an attempt to enter Tibet proper, still officially off-limits to foreigners at the time. (They were turned back by a border patrol near the forlorn garrison town of Golmud.) Anne and I continued on to Xinjiang in China's far northwest, a purportedly autonomous region inhabited largely by Turkic-speaking Muslim peoples such as the Uighurs, Kazakhs, Uzbeks, Kirghiz, and Tajiks.

Our first stop in Xinjiang was the regional market city of Turfan, situated hundreds of feet below sea level in the Turfan Depression, the lowest point in the entire Asian continent. Crushed by hammer-blow heat routinely exceeding 110 degrees Fahrenheit, Turfan is mercifully cooled by an ingenious irrigation system that supplies the city and neighboring countryside with year-round glacial runoff from the high Tian Shan ("Heavenly Mountains") peaks to the north. We passed two pleasant days in the town, fending off the cruel August sun with cold Xinjiang Beer in the courtyard of the Turfan guesthouse, where we spent long afternoons exchanging tales with other Western travelers. It was here that we formed a lasting friendship with French Canadians Pierre and Danielle Daigneault and their extraordinarily bright son Yann, who by age seven would be fluent in French, English, Mandarin Chinese, and Cantonese. Together we visited the vast ruined city of Gaochang, the Astana Tombs with their mummified human remains, and the Bezeklik "Thousand Buddha Caves," vandalized by Muslim and Red Guard zealots who'd painstakingly scratched out the faces of every single Buddha painted on the cave walls. Anne and I then traveled on to the drab provincial capital of Urumqi, the tourist-choked beauty spot of Heaven Lake, and the lovely alpine high country of the Tian Shan mountains, where we spent two nights in a traditional Kazakh yurt in the company of Pierre, Danielle, and Yann.

Xinjiang is Chinese in name and governance only, a land of mosques, melons, and mutton kebabs where the ruled far outnumber the rulers. Thousands of kilometers removed from the Han cultural heartland, the region's Chinese populace is a motley assortment of frontier soldiers, political exiles, miners, oilmen, and hardy entrepreneurs, few of whom live in this arid landscape by choice. Relations are tense between the Muslim majority and the growing numbers of unwelcome Chinese settlers, viewed with some justification as the vanguard of a Beijing-orchestrated social engineering plot. Incidences of ethnic violence are increasingly common, and in recent years a Uighur separatist movement has gathered momentum, inspired in part by the newly won independence of their cousins across the border in the former Soviet republics.

The uneasy coexistence of the Chinese with Xinjiang's native peoples dates back more than 2,000 years to the earliest days of the Silk Road, when the powerful Han Dynasty extended its dominion over the region in an effort to secure a vital east-west trade route. The Silk Road proved to be a conduit not only for material goods but also for religious and artistic interchange, most significantly the introduction of Buddhism into China from India. One enduring result of this cultural synergy was the subsequent development of

Chinese music. Surprisingly, in a culture so loath to admit any outside influence, Chinese scholars readily acknowledge the formative impact of foreign music—especially that of cultures to which China was linked by the Silk Road—on Chinese musical tradition. This cross-pollination is most apparent in the standard "Chinese" musical instruments, most of which were actually imported long ago from Persia and the Middle East and then modified to suit local purposes. One such example is the Chinese *pipa*, a common teardrop-shaped stringed instrument that is descended from the same ancestor as the European lute and North African *oud*. China's *yangqin* (hammered dulcimer) likewise has its origin in the similar Persian *santur*.

To this day, Chinese aesthetes praise the music of Xinjiang for its vigor, virtuosity, and sensuality. In its unadulterated form, as in the largely improvised *maqams* of the Uighurs, the music of northwest China exhibits a dynamism and spontaneity rarely found in the studied Confucian classicism that pervades much traditional Chinese music. But like most ethnic minority art forms in China, the music of present-day Xinjiang has been steadily diluted by Chinese and other outside influences. Although relatively pure strains of traditional music still persist in isolated mountain villages, visitors are more likely to

*The ruined city of Gaochang in Xinjiang (Dennis Rea)*

hear dispassionate, government-sanctioned song and dance troupes like the one we heard performing for tourists in the courtyard of the Turfan Guesthouse. Night after night these bored Uighur musicians and dancers, clad in exaggeratedly "authentic" costumes, mechanically perform the type of Silk Road clichés the Chinese have come to expect of them, in a sort of Asian Wild West show. Troupes like these have long been a fixture in the traveling culture fairs organized by the Chinese government to promote the dubious notion of national unity, but they ultimately serve only to reinforce longstanding stereotypes.

The traditional music of China's Han majority didn't fare much better than that of the Uighurs under communist rule. Like the nation itself, Chinese music for centuries successfully assimilated elements of other Asian cultures while retaining its own distinct identity. But China's eventual encounter with European classical music dramatically upended deeply rooted musical traditions, as the alien science of functional harmony clashed with the essentially non-harmonic methodology of Chinese musical practice. When confronted with the imposing edifice of European music theory, many Chinese musicians dismissed their own tradition as comparatively unsophisticated. By the late 1800s China's national instruments were falling out of favor with the musical elite, casualties of the country's love affair with that embodiment of Western musical hegemony, the piano, and to a slightly lesser degree the violin. Despite the best efforts of propagandists to outlaw Western art forms during the Cultural Revolution, this obsession with European music continues to this day and remains the focus of formal music education in China.

While China has produced an impressive number of virtuoso performers in the European tradition, the national infatuation with European music has also spawned an unfortunate forced fusion of Chinese folk melodies with Western orchestration. Though a source of great pride to ardent nationalists, such lightweight, European-influenced works as the "Yellow River Concerto" and "The Butterfly

Lovers," with their puerile patriotic melodies and cloying "101 Strings" romanticism, combine the worst of both worlds. Not until the emergence in the 1980s of fiercely imaginative "New Tide" composers such as Tan Dun and Guo Wenjing did China's embrace of Western musical values produce a mutually enriching synthesis of the two traditions, rather than mere pastiche.

Another factor in the decline of traditional music was the official cultural policy of the Chinese Communist Party. For decades after the 1949 communist revolution, music's sole purpose was to be a transmitter of political and moral propaganda. Party ideologues condemned China's rich classical and folk music heritage as representative of feudalist "old thinking," and individual initiative was subsumed in the long march toward a utopian socialist society. The only officially sanctioned musical genres in the post-Liberation period were politically correct socialist anthems, Madame Mao's dour revolutionary operas, and feel-good ditties extolling the praises of the Motherland. Not surprisingly, the public never really warmed to utilitarian music that was as dull as day-old bread. Only after Deng Xiaoping relaxed constraints on popular culture in the late 1970s did Chinese music begin to wriggle out of its ideological straitjacket. Traditional music performance and research resumed, romantic love songs were again tolerated, and foreign styles such as rock and disco first appeared in China, engendering new East-West fusions. Among the more bizarre hybrids was a series of recordings of Cultural Revolution songs set to a thumping disco beat, with singers belting out such incongruous lyrics as

> *Chairman Mao's works are my favorites;*
> *I scrutinize them thousands of times.*
> *Carefully understanding those profound theories*
> *Makes me feel so warm in my heart.*
> *It feels like a punctual rain in dry land,*
> *Dewdrops hanging on seedlings.*
> *Chairman Mao's dewdrops nourished me.*
> *I'm full of energy working for our revolution.*

Simultaneously an expression of nostalgia for the bad old days and a sly poke at the Party, the Maoist disco records sold briskly throughout the late 1980s and early 90s.

At the cusp of the 1990s, China was at a major crossroads not only politically and economically but also musically. So where did a clueless Western musician like me fit into the big picture? Was I a guitar-slinging Johnny Appleseed sowing seeds of musical liberation, or the unwitting agent of a global conspiracy to erode Chinese mores with sex, drugs, and rock and roll?

Our final excursion of the summer was to the Wolong Giant Panda Reserve in the thickly forested mountains of northwestern Sichuan's Aba Tibetan-Qiang Autonomous Prefecture. Jointly administered by the Chinese government and the World Wide Fund for Nature, Wolong was established in 1975 to protect one of the last relatively unspoiled areas of giant panda habitat. Situated astride the natural boundary separating two distinct biogeographic regions, the reserve encompasses an incredibly rich and diverse ecosystem ranging from luxuriant subtropical forests to windswept alpine uplands to the arrow bamboo groves on which the panda depends for its survival. The sanctuary also contains a breeding center that has played a central role in stabilizing the threatened panda population, which declined precipitously in the twentieth century due to poaching and human encroachment. Other endangered species that find sanctuary in Wolong include the lesser panda, snow leopard, clouded leopard, golden monkey, wild yak, and takin, a hulking, rarely seen creature that resembles a cross between a mountain goat and a moose.

We had long wanted to visit Wolong but had been deterred by government restrictions on access by foreigners. While the restrictions were ostensibly aimed at limiting tourist traffic to the panda reserve, they were also meant to block unauthorized travel to Tibet via a little-known back road that passes through Wolong before climbing steeply onto the Tibetan Plateau. Tellingly, this secret backdoor to Tibet did not appear on any of the Chinese-made maps sold to foreign travelers, though it was clearly indicated on detailed Chinese-language maps.

Earlier that summer, Anne and I had complained to our Chinese friend Carmen about the difficulty of visiting Wolong. Carmen suggested that the three of us travel there with her brother, whose status as a Chengdu police lieutenant would presumably guarantee us admittance to the restricted area. We accepted her offer gratefully, appreciative of the police for a change.

On a gray September morning, the four of us set out for Wolong, looking suitably official in the jeep her brother had borrowed from the Chengdu police force. After about an hour of driving, we left the cultivated fields and paddies of the Chengdu Plain behind and began a steady ascent into the mist-draped Qionglai Mountains, which culminate in the jaw-dropping 20,000-foot spike of Mount Siguniang, just 80 miles west of urban Chengdu. Elderly Chengdu residents wistfully recall a time when the white profile of Siguniang could be descried from the city's taller structures, before industrial murk had obliterated all sight of the noble peak's presence.

The road turned up the narrow valley of the rushing Pitiao River and quickly deteriorated into a barely passable track riddled with chuckholes and treacherous muddy pools. Even the police jeep had difficulty making progress in these conditions, and it took us the better part of the day to cover the 75 miles from Chengdu to the tiny hamlet that contained the reserve's only guesthouse.

No sooner did we park the mud-spattered jeep than the local constable strode up and brusquely demanded to know what business our party—and particularly the two foreigners—had in Wolong. Did we have a government permit? Carmen's brother drew himself up in his olive-green Chengdu Police uniform and explained that Anne and I were American teachers from KeDa who wanted to visit the reserve. Determined to stake out his jurisdiction, the constable stubbornly insisted that we present evidence of official clearance, which of course we didn't have. The two cops soon became embroiled in a turf war that quickly escalated into a red-faced shouting match.

Although the battle of wills was eventually won by Carmen's brother, who clearly outranked his backwoods counterpart, the defeated constable managed to save some face by charging us an outrageous 70 RMB for a night's lodging in the austere guesthouse, about 10 times what it normally would have cost. It was always an eye-opener to see how ill at ease Chinese citizens became when foreigners arrived unannounced in a rural locale. I felt sorry for Carmen and her brother, who were obviously finding their foreign guests more trouble than they had bargained for.

That evening we sat down to a simple country-style meal with the dozen or so local residents in a rustic semi-enclosed structure that served as the village store, restaurant, and social hub. Before long someone broke out a bottle of liquor, and the afternoon's altercation was quickly forgotten. Several rounds of toasts cemented the budding friendship between the big-city cop and his erstwhile adversary, who remained inseparable for the rest of our stay.

We awoke the next morning to a brilliant blue sky and a refreshingly crisp mountain breeze. Yesterday's mists had lifted, revealing a series of steep verdant ridges converging on the lofty Tibetan highlands to the west. After a bite of breakfast with the now-cordial villagers, Carmen's brother dropped us off at a hiking trail a few miles further up the road and then returned to the village to hang out with his new pal the constable. The rest of us headed up the path into an area of prime panda habitat. The trail rapidly gained elevation, at one point traversing a long, dripping tunnel through a stony mountain buttress. Well aware that our chances of sighting a panda in the wild were microscopic, we nonetheless imagined that we could sense the secretive animals' presence in the surrounding forest. It wasn't hard to see why the pandas had taken refuge in this wilderness of improbable pinnacles clothed in tangled verdure—it would have taken a human an hour to bushwhack a few dozen meters off the trail.

At length we turned back and descended to the road. Rather than wait for Carmen's brother to return for us, we set off on foot in the direction of the village, from time to time passing homesteads of the Qiang people who inhabit the rugged ranges of the Sichuan-Tibet frontier. Driven into ever more remote valleys over the centuries by Chinese expansion, the Qiang minority eke out a meager living by cultivating small plots in the narrow valley bottoms or on terraces cut into the mountainsides, and by gathering medicinal herbs, roots, and (sometimes illegal) animal parts for sale to the Chinese. We paused to admire the solid, attractive Qiang homes, constructed of meticulously fitted flagstones and sturdy log beams.

As we neared one such house, a young Qiang woman in traditional blue dress approached and graciously invited us in for tea. While we welcomed the opportunity to observe the Qiang lifestyle, the scene that awaited us inside was rather disturbing to our urban sensibilities. The interior of the house was in disarray, its hard-packed dirt floor strewn with animal feces, gnawed bones, and offal. As our hostess prepared us some watery tea, we watched in horror as a chicken ate out of the same bowl as her baby boy and then turned its attention to pecking at the child's excrement. Our hostess took a seat opposite us and began relating a pitiful tale of woe. A mother of four, she had run afoul of local government officials for violating China's strict one-child policy, and the resultant fines and decreased rations had reduced her to a state of grinding poverty. Her husband was gone for weeks at a time collecting herbs on the mountain slopes, leaving her to manage the chaotic household on her own. With tears trickling down her cheeks, she voiced bitter regret over having had too many children, though it was unclear what responsibility the men in her life bore for her predicament. Unnerved by her plight, we thanked her for the tea and gave her a bit of money to ease her burden, deeply saddened to see this attractive woman cut down so early in life. Her neighbors looked askance at us as we left her dwelling, as though we had been tainted by our association with the village pariah.

Our stay in Wolong concluded with a visit to the panda breeding center, where we enjoyed the privilege of seeing several of the strikingly beautiful animals at close range. I couldn't resist the urge to stroke one adult panda's fur as it leaned against the bars of its enclosure, a rare honor indeed. We then took leave of Wolong's therapeutic stillness and bumped our way back down the rugged road to teeming metropolitan Chengdu.

# CHAPTER 9

# WE WISH YOU HAPPY

After our summer travels I found myself deluged with requests to play guitar in settings ranging from informal parties to riverside pubs to the imposing Worker's Cultural Palace. Despite lingering post-Tiananmen tensions, I was even granted permission to organize two wildly successful concerts for the seriously demoralized students at our university. All this exposure inevitably brought me to the attention of the regional media, who were eager to capitalize on the novelty of a foreign guitar player in their midst.

In late fall, state-operated Sichuan Radio invited me to their studio to make a multi-track recording that was later broadcast throughout the province. Just before Chinese New Year, I was asked back to perform in the station's holiday gala, improvising with nationally renowned *erhu* player Zhu Ling on the theme song to the hit television series *Dream of the Red Chamber*, based on one of the enduring classics of Chinese literature. I was astonished to learn that an estimated 10 million Sichuan residents listened to our performance. Another musical collaboration, with the Chengdu-based composer Huang Qiang on his electronic suite "Impressions of the East," was heard by an even larger national radio audience. I couldn't believe how many people my music was reaching. Despite being a most unlikely candidate, I had somehow stumbled into the role of musical ambassador, introducing impossibly vast audiences to jazz, art rock, and other novel foreign musical genres. Representing these creative music traditions was both a great privilege and a weighty responsibility. Forget teaching English—from now on, propagating music would be my top priority.

Amid all this whirlwind music-making, Anne and I somehow found time to get married. We'd been planning to tie the knot for some time and thought it would be romantic to plight our troth in exotic Cathay. We may well have waited longer had we foreseen the maddening obstacle course we would have to negotiate before obtaining our marriage license.

Hoping to avoid entanglement in Byzantine communist bureaucracy, we enlisted the help of a university official, who contacted the appropriate government ministry to determine proper procedure for foreigners getting married in China. Our go-between reported back with a list of paperwork we would need, and on the appointed day in late December we were driven to the marriage bureau with documents in hand, excited to think that in a few minutes we would officially be wed.

Our spirits sank quickly when we walked into the marriage bureau office, a dim, depressing cement cubicle occupied by a handful of bored functionaries reading newspapers at their desks. A scowling female official looked up at us in annoyance and asked us to state our business. When we explained that we had come for our marriage license, the woman brusquely demanded our papers, gave them a cursory glance, and then irritably informed us that we were missing certain vital documents. We would have to obtain said papers, including an affidavit from the U.S. consulate, and come back another day. Crestfallen, Anne and I left the office with our embarrassed chaperone, still single.

The next day we returned with the requested documents, only to be told that we lacked some additional required items, setting off a new paper chase. On our third visit to the marriage bureau we were again turned down over yet another minor technicality. It appeared that the heartless bureaucrats were going out of their way to trip us up merely for their own amusement. On the fourth day we were dispatched to a medical examiner's office to acquire a clean bill of health; during my checkup, an elderly nurse squeezed my testicles and assured Anne with a grin that there were "no problems" in that department. On the *fifth* day I walked into the marriage office ready to commit homicide, but this time our tormentor unceremoniously stamped our application, forced a smile, and congratulated us on being married. Though our wedding was hardly the romantic consummation we had imagined, we had succeeded in becoming the first foreign couple to be married in Sichuan Province since the 1949 communist revolution.

In January my beer-drinking buddy Michael Liu invited me to spend Chinese New Year with his family in their hometown of Zigong, a small city 200 kilometers south of Chengdu that is famous for its wealth of dinosaur fossils and extensive salt deposits. Such an invitation was a rare honor, so I accepted with gratitude. In those days, foreigners generally weren't allowed to stay in Chinese homes, but Michael's father, the influential head of a large factory, somehow managed to secure permission to have me as a houseguest.

The day before Chinese New Year the two of us took a train to Zigong, passing through the wavelike bamboo-fringed hillocks of the green Sichuan Basin. Now and then Michael would purchase snacks and beer from vendors on station platforms along the way, and by the time we pulled into Zigong I was already feeling uncomfortably full. The moment we arrived at Michael's home his mother began plying me with more snacks and pastries, which I could hardly refuse without offending her. Meanwhile, preparations were underway for a serious banquet on my behalf. That evening the family and several guests gathered around the table for a truly magnificent array of Sichuanese delicacies—fiery *mapo tofu*, wok-seared green beans, crispy barbecued duck, and much more—followed by endless bottles of beer. At midnight we tuned in Sichuan Radio and listened to my prerecorded Chinese New Year broadcast, which greatly elevated my stature in the eyes of my hosts. I went to bed feeling like someone had inflated my gut with a tire pump.

In the morning I awoke to the sound of Michael's mother summoning me to breakfast. I groaned inwardly, for a battle was already raging in my distended belly. At length I arose, waddled into the dining room, and tried to excuse myself graciously from breakfast, explaining that I didn't normally eat first thing in the morning. But Michael's mom wouldn't hear of it, no doubt thinking I was just being polite. Panicked at the thought of abusing my stomach any further, I committed the cardinal sin of saying that I felt slightly ill, hoping that Mrs. Liu wouldn't think I was insulting her cooking. She shrugged this off with a laugh, insisting that I eat just a little bit "for my health." I finally caved in. Her idea of a little bit turned out to be a huge bowl of heavy, glutinous rice dumplings.

As I nibbled slowly on a single massive dumpling, the family urged me to hurry because we were due shortly at the home of a Mr. Zhang, who was preparing a special New Year's banquet for me. A colleague of Mr. Liu's, Mr. Zhang presumably wanted to share in the prestige of entertaining the foreign guest and had gone all-out to assemble a dazzling cornucopia of Sichuanese dishes. Powerless to extricate myself from this commitment, I went along meekly to Mr. Zhang's and sat down at his table feeling like I was pregnant with twins. In a supreme exercise of willpower, I managed to swallow a few meager mouthfuls without gagging. Though I took pains to thank Mr. Zhang and his wife profusely and compliment them on their fantastic cooking, I could see that he felt I was snubbing him by eating so little of his expensive repast.

I counted the seconds until the meal and toasts concluded and then hoisted myself out of my chair and headed back to the Lius' apartment, hoping to recover for a few hours. Alas, within minutes, Mr. Liu was handing me my coat and saying we mustn't be late for our appointment at the home of Mr. Zhou, another of his colleagues—who was hosting a New Year's feast in my honor! I endured this second banquet in even greater agony, hardly touching the Zhou family's costly spread. Now I knew what it felt like to be a plump, force-fed Beijing duck. I left Zigong mortified at having embarrassed my hosts by spurning their hospitality, even though I truly couldn't have downed another morsel. Unbelievably, I gained a good 10 pounds over my three days in Zigong. When I returned to the Panda Palace in Chengdu, the *fuwuyuan* laughed out loud to see how I'd swelled. Anne told me that she'd never seen a human being balloon so rapidly.

*Anne in Tibet, 1989*

# CHAPTER 10

# Ain't Nothin' but a Hongbao

On an overcast afternoon in January 1990, my teenage acquaintance Xiao Fei turned up at my door with a longhaired fellow named Chu Fei, who played drums for the Beijing rock group Yinhuochong ("Firefly Band"). Xiao Fei explained that the band was in town to play two concerts at the Chengdu sports arena with the famous Chinese pop singer Zhang Xing. Xiao Fei had befriended Chu Fei years earlier in Beijing and evidently wanted to score some points by showing off the American guitarist to his rocker pal.

With his retro Mao cap and Artful Dodger insouciance, Xiao Fei typified a new generation of hip Chinese youths who'd traded in their Little Red Books for rock and roll. He was my earliest link to the "Chinarock" scene then emerging in Beijing, and by introducing me to Zhang Xing and the music of rock legend Cui Jian, he unwittingly set in motion a series of events that would have life-changing consequences for me and many others.

At Xiao Fei's urging I gave Chu Fei an impromptu guitar recital in my apartment. The grinning drummer listened for a few minutes and then insisted that I accompany him to the Tibet Hotel to play for Zhang Xing and the rest of the band. Intrigued, I shouldered my guitar case and walked out to the Ring Road with the two young men to flag down a taxi.

Zhang Xing—sometimes known as Zhang Hang—was quite the dandy with his impeccably tailored suit, slicked-back hair, and stylish dark glasses. (The sunglasses were a Zhang Xing trademark; he rarely removed them, even indoors or after dark.) He carried himself with the superior air of a Hong Kong sophisticate and delighted in displaying his wealth, conspicuously brandishing an inch-thick wad of U.S., Japanese, Taiwanese, and Chinese currency when dining out. He thought nothing of spending on lunch what most families earned in a month, and his entourage always included a retinue of stunning young ladies. It was no wonder the government considered him a bad element.

The progenitor of Chinese rock first took up the guitar as a teen in his native Shanghai at the tail end of the Cultural Revolution, a time when anti-foreign sentiment was running high and the guitar was still condemned as a Trojan Horse carrying a deadly cultural

contagion—which of course it proved to be. Zhang Xing's flirtation with Western pop music didn't sit well with the local culture cops, and he claims that the police confiscated and destroyed several of his guitars during that period.

When China's cultural climate thawed somewhat under the relatively progressive leadership of Deng Xiaoping in the late 1970s, the government relaxed control over artistic expression, within limits. Creative impulses that had been stifled during the Cultural Revolution found vent in autobiographical "wound literature," the breakthrough cinema of such "Fifth Generation" filmmakers as Zhang Yimou and Chen Kaige, the experimental music of academic "New Tide" composers, and Western-influenced popular music. It was around this time that the *tongsu* ("mass music") industry arose to fill the emotional void left by the Cultural Revolution and its monotonous, sexless paeans to Chairman Mao, socialism, and the Motherland. The *tongsu* craze, which dominates the Chinese popular music market to this day, was catalyzed by the best-selling hits of charismatic Taiwanese songstress Deng Lijun (also known as Teresa Teng), whose girlish bubblegum love songs fell like rain on an emotionally parched populace. Soon singers in the mold of Deng Lijun were all the rage, flooding the airwaves with glossy chart-toppers and playing sellout concerts in huge arenas from Nanning to Harbin. But the *tongsu* star's glamorous public image belied a life of virtual servitude to Party overseers, who supervised every last detail of a singer's repertoire, lyrics, and performance style. Though state censors generally tolerated softcore love songs, mild social criticism, and even lighthearted parodies of Cultural Revolution-era anthems, *tongsu* essentially remained true to its prescribed function as music for "the people"—that is, until the libidinous Zhang Xing exploded onto the scene.

In the early 1980s, a young Zhang Xing sang and played guitar on a Shanghai TV talent show and won first prize for his erotically charged performance. Over the next few days thousands of guitars were sold in the Shanghai metropolitan area. The young sensation soon attained national fame and scored a number of guitar-driven commercial hits such as "The Green Plains," "Ashi," and "Too Late," securing his place as Mainland China's first homegrown rock icon. By the end of the decade he had reportedly sold more records than any musician in Chinese history.

By anything-goes Western standards, Zhang Xing's repertoire of revved-up Taiwan and Hong Kong pop ballads was laughably tame, but his swoony love songs provided heady titillation to a public bored with bland socialist entertainment. He was in fact an excellent singer, possessed of an artfully nuanced, caressing voice that I found genuinely moving. Before long he became the most commercially successful entertainer in China, earning upwards of 5,000 RMB per concert (about US$1,000 at the time), roughly 50 times the monthly income of the average citizen in the 1980s. A charter member of China's neo-capitalist stratosphere, Zhang Xing's hubris eventually proved to be his undoing. Giddy with celebrity, he affected a flamboyant lifestyle and flaunted his profligate sexual relationships, becoming something of a tabloid character in the public eye and earning the disapproval of a regime that viewed him as an unwholesome role model for Chinese youth and the emergence of rock and roll in general as a threat to societal stability.

The government eventually grew so annoyed at the singer's spreading influence that they banned his music outright and in 1985 sentenced him to an eight-year prison term on a contrived statutory rape charge, a rite of symbolic public execution that the Chinese call "killing the chicken to scare the monkeys." Zhang Xing insisted that the incident amounted to nothing more than a jealous girlfriend blowing the whistle on one of his affairs. Whatever the sordid details, the Western press picked up the story and made much of China's persecution of rock music, restriction of free speech, and summary justice. Presumably as a result of this embarrassing negative publicity, the Chinese government released Zhang Xing three years into his sentence. He was in the middle of his comeback tour when I played guitar for him in his Chengdu hotel room.

No sooner did I give Zhang Xing a brief demonstration of my guitar playing than he asked me to join his band for their two concerts at the Chengdu sports arena—in just two days! Dumbfounded, I declined at first, stammering that I didn't know the material, but he would have none of it, and the band—Chu Fei, guitarist Gong

Ming, bassist Xie Ning, and keyboardist Chen Ping—reassured me that the simple tunes would be a snap for me to learn. I started to warm to the absurd proposition; if nothing else, my cameo turn with a Chinese pop star would make a great yarn to tell over beers back in the States. So I dismissed my initial misgivings and accepted Zhang Xing's offer, but only on the condition that I would have ample time to rehearse the songs with the band.

As it turned out, we rehearsed only once, and the band was far more interested in learning my songs than in teaching me their set. The following day I found myself on stage in front of 5,000 people, blindly improvising my way through 10 Mandarin pop songs I had scarcely heard before. I had to listen to the first few bars of each tune before I even knew which one we were playing.

I had often wondered what it would be like to play in front of such a massive audience, and I half-expected to be paralyzed with anxiety. Yet to my immense relief I discovered that the blinding stage lights obliterated all sight of the crowd, allowing me to relax enough to focus on the alien repertoire as though we were playing in a large, empty rehearsal room.

The concerts were full-blown, Las Vegas–style extravaganzas, complete with ritual flower presentations and dancing girls decked out in Cultural Revolution garb. A highlight of the set was Yinhuochong's rocked-out rendering of the old Maoist anthem "Tai Yang Zui Hong." As a concession to their foreign guest, the band also played my Middle Eastern–flavored instrumental workout, "Hot Pot," which went down fairly well with the crowd, despite the fact that the emcee bellowed greetings throughout most of the song.

Apparently satisfied with my efforts, Zhang Xing asked me to accompany the band to Chongqing for four more concerts in that city's sports arena. By now I was in danger of getting in way over my head due to the inadequacy of my spoken Chinese. Thankfully, a friend of Anne's, Tang Lei, stepped in and assumed the role of my manager. Tang Lei was married to the artist Zhang Xiaogang, now one of the leading Chinese painters in the world, and functioned as an unofficial agent for radical artists in Sichuan and Yunnan Provinces. She possessed a diplomatic manner, shrewd managerial instincts, a passion for advancing creative art in China, and an understanding of the nuances of Chinese thinking that I could never hope to share. Tang Lei skillfully steered me through the rest of the Zhang Xing experience and went on to act as my manager through all my subsequent musical endeavors in China, for which I am ever grateful. I would not have accomplished half as much without her guidance. Years later, Tang Lei would find herself at the center of a musical renaissance in Chengdu, earning the affectionate sobriquet "Mother of Chengdu Rock."

In Chongqing, Zhang Xing wisely used me in fewer songs, instead giving me a solo feature in which I performed Central Asian Uighur music on electric guitar, much to the audience's bewilderment. But by the end of our stint in Chongqing I was feeling utterly foolish playing inane pop tunes that I wouldn't have been caught dead performing in my own country. It was the novelty of the situation that had appealed to me, not the music. Yet I was grateful to Yinhuochong for performing my music in public, and I admired Zhang Xing for taking the political risk of including me in his program, though he no doubt profited from having an exotic ornament in his backup band.

Most importantly, my experience with Zhang Xing opened my eyes to the existence of a highly developed pop music subculture in China, something I had never expected to find in this supposedly repressive communist country. As in the West, the scene came complete with sleazy promoters, leather-clad backstage groupies, hangers-on, posers, and big money. Throughout our stay in Chongqing we were served three gigantic meals daily in the hotel banquet hall, along with all the beer and expensive *Wuliangye* liquor we could stand. Most of the food went uneaten and was simply thrown away after the meals—and to think that my mother had shamed me into cleaning my plate by admonishing me to "think of the poor starving Chinese."

Little did I expect that my chance encounter with pop-culture royalty in the person of Zhang Xing would change my life dramatically from that moment onward. After many years of making obscure music in the shadows, I now had to deal with the novel experience of being an overnight celebrity—in communist China, no less.

No sooner did news spread of my appearance with the famous Zhang Xing than the students and faculty at the university began to view me in a different light. Friends and acquaintances crowded our apartment to vicariously partake of the buzz, and skeptics who'd questioned my stature as a musician (no doubt wondering why any accomplished player would be teaching English in Chengdu) quickly changed their tune when told of my stint with the superstar crooner. My reputation was cemented a few days after the Zhang Xing shows when Yinhuochong made a surprise appearance at a concert I staged at our university, to the audible delight of students still demoralized by the events of the previous June.

My rising prominence wasn't confined to the campus community, either. Our apartment soon became a salon of sorts for a growing contingent of longhaired poets, painters, and other bohemian types from all over the city. (Although university officials frowned on such visits, slipping a bottle of beer to the night watchman always did the trick.) On my errands about town, complete strangers would point me out on the street and play air guitar. Touring Chinese pop stars such as the then-fashionable Sun Guoqing would look me up when passing through Chengdu. Local and regional media contacted me to arrange appearances, and even the U.S. consulate took a heightened if bemused interest in my activities. Invitations began pouring in to play in such far-flung locales as Shandong Province on the east coast and Xinjiang in the Central Asian desert, for fees that would dwarf my paltry teacher's salary. For someone who had been resigned to laboring quietly at the margins of the music industry, it was exhilarating to say the least.

It seemed that my dream of being a self-supporting creative

musician was finally within my grasp, under outlandish circumstances that I scarcely could have dreamed up. Yet tempting as the prospect was, my teaching contract was quickly drawing to a close and my visa was due to expire. Even though university officials made the unprecedented move of extending my visa for three months so that I could wrap up my musical activities, it was nearly time for Anne and me to pull up stakes and move on to Taiwan as we had long planned.

# CHAPTER 11

# SHADOW IN DREAMS

Toward the end of my stay in Chengdu I received a visit from Yang Shichun, a producer for the regional branch of the state-run China Record Company, which virtually monopolized commercial music production and distribution throughout the country. To my astonishment, Yang told me that he had heard me play and wanted to produce an album of my music for China Records. Needless to say, I was thrilled at the proposition; after all, how many foreign musicians were ever given the opportunity to publish their music in China? However, I felt it was only fair to caution Yang that releasing an album of my odd instrumental music would likely amount to fiscal suicide. I wondered whether he had really listened carefully to my music, or if he was only interested in me because I was a foreign curiosity.

I asked Yang if I would be free to select the material for the record and arrange it as I wished. He assured me that I would have complete artistic control over the content, provided that I make one small concession to popular tastes by including a piece of "light" music on the album. When I asked what he had in mind, Yang cited the example of Richard Clayderman, the sentimental French pianist whose lightweight easy-listening albums were all the rage in 1980s China. Richard Clayderman! I cringed to think that my musicianship could be so completely misunderstood. With a sigh, I told Yang that I didn't think I was the right person for what he was proposing.

Surprised at my reluctance, he asked me to think it over for a few days before giving him my decision.

Two days later Yang returned to the Panda Palace with a fresh proposal. Conceding that Richard Clayderman wasn't an appropriate model for a player with my background, he asked if I would agree to include a guitar adaptation of the popular Beethoven piano tune "Für Elise," a ubiquitous piece of background music in China at the time. Otherwise, he explained, it would be very difficult for China Records to market an entire album of weird music by an unknown foreign instrumentalist. I didn't like "Für Elise" much better than I liked Clayderman, but I assented, thinking it was a small price to pay for the privilege of making a record in China. Yang agreed to let me arrange the tune however I liked, and the deal was done.

The recording that was to become *Shadow in Dreams* was made over four days at China Records' Chengdu studio, a surprisingly low-tech facility that was so cold I could see my breath while playing. The session was plagued with technical breakdowns, electrical noise, and faulty power cords, and was altogether too hurried—in other words, a typical recording date in the PRC. For material, I augmented a selection of my guitar works with an electric arrangement of the traditional *erhu* piece "Hong Bo Qu," duets with guitarist Zhao Xiong and pianist Yang Chenggang, and a multilayered synthesizer piece I had written years before. As the session progressed, I deliberately avoided mentioning "Für Elise" in the hope that it would somehow get lost in the shuffle, but on my final day in the studio Yang drew me aside and made it clear that I would not be paid unless I recorded the Beethoven track. I sucked up my pride and honored my commitment, but I got the last laugh in the end when, much to Yang's chagrin, I managed to disfigure "Für Elise" almost beyond recognition with the help of cardboard string mutes, knitting needles, and cheap electronic processing. I wasn't surprised to find the piece heavily edited on the final release.

*Shadow in Dreams* was released in summer 1990 on cassette, as record players were scarce and CDs had not yet arrived in China. According to some sources it was the first album ever made by a foreigner for China Records, an assertion I have never verified and rather doubt. The awkward album title was the result of a compromise with the record company, who wanted something "romantic" and even suggested naming it "Dreams of Annie," a pointed reference to John Denver. The cassette cover displayed my blue-tinted face, half in shadow, looking every bit the foreign devil. The music itself was far more conservative than I would have liked and involved

the regrettable use of an electronic drum machine, but it was the best I could manage under the circumstances and was certainly unlike anything else produced by the label. Yang had hoped to sell a few hundred units and recoup his expenses, but to my everlasting astonishment *Shadow in Dreams* went on to sell an estimated 40,000 copies throughout China, generating about 200,000 RMB (roughly US$40,000) in sales for the record company. Of this, I received approximately US$500, which nevertheless was considerably more than many of the label's star artists were normally paid. The record was even listed among the 10 best releases of 1990 by the

Communist Party newspaper *China Youth Daily*. Years later, strangers still approached me after shows to tell me how much they enjoyed my record. One fellow even credited *Shadow in Dreams* with inspiring him to take up music as an avocation, one of the most meaningful compliments I've ever received.

My final undertaking before leaving China was a television special produced by Chengdu TV, *The Gitar* (sic) *Music of Dennis Rea*. The program showed me playing guitar in a TV studio decorated with faux-psychedelic geometric props; visiting Chengdu's historic attractions; struggling to ingest slippery rice noodles from a bubbling hot pot filled with whole pig brains, cow tripe, and other sweetmeats; and rowing a silly little boat in a polluted canal. I found the shtick extremely embarrassing but was a virtual captive of the TV crew. The footage never fails to induce howls of laughter from my friends and family.

# CHAPTER 12

# THE GANG OF FORMOSA

In April 1990, Anne and I left China for Taiwan on the recommendation of Brad Locke, an American teacher we'd befriended in Chengdu. Anne wanted to continue her Chinese language studies in a more agreeable environment, and we both hoped to find better-paying work as English teachers in capitalist Taiwan, having exhausted our paltry savings in China. In Chengdu, our salaries had amounted to a whopping US$125 per month; by contrast, foreign English teachers in Taiwan routinely earned US$20 per *hour*. We were also curious to see what direction Chinese culture had taken under a non-socialist political system.

Ever since the late 1940s, when the remnants of Generalissimo Chiang Kai-Shek's nationalist forces had fled to and imposed their rule on Taiwan in the wake of China's communist revolution, the People's Republic of China (PRC) and Chiang's Republic of China (ROC) had traveled along radically different courses. While the PRC endured a devastating series of famines, political purges, and ruinous mass movements, the ROC survived and prospered for decades basically by U.S. fiat, its sovereignty protected by American warships and its economy propped up by U.S. dollars. Despite being left in the lurch by President Jimmy Carter when he restored U.S. ties with mainland China in 1976, by the 1980s this once-sleepy island of pineapple and sugarcane plantations had joined the ranks of the world's economic success stories, boasting an astonishing US$80 billion in foreign capital and an estimated quarter of the globe's gold reserves. Taiwan's extraordinary economic transformation earned it a place alongside Hong Kong, South Korea, and Singapore as one of Asia's "Four Little Dragons."

Conditioned as we were to the drabness of everyday life in Chengdu, we found ourselves overwhelmed at first by the brightly lit, high-speed commercial culture that was Taiwan. The ROC of the early 1990s was a nation of BMWs and Benzes, Madonna and MTV, computer whiz kids and import-export tycoons, and its institutions betrayed a pronounced Japanese influence. The already overcrowded island—home to a populace the size of Canada's jammed into a land area the size of Vancouver Island—was awash in development, with multilane superhighways, oversized skyscrapers (including for a time the world's tallest), and sprawling high-tech industrial parks sprouting up wherever space permitted. While the underside of Taiwan's economic boom was apparent in its world-class traffic snarls and horribly poisoned rivers—I once spotted a dead bear on a gravel bar in the Tanshui River, right in the heart of cosmopolitan Taipei—there was no denying that the Taiwanese now enjoyed a far higher standard of living than their less fortunate cousins across the Formosa Strait in China.

Politically, the ROC was still officially at war with the PRC, and despite all empirical evidence to the contrary, the living fossils who made up much of the ROC legislature still doggedly insisted that the Kuomintang (KMT), or Nationalist Party, was the rightful ruler of all China. Indeed, some of the aged KMT politicians were so oblivious to geopolitical reality that they still represented mainland provinces such as Chichihar and Jehol that had long since vanished from the map. But the government's stated aim to reunite with the motherland on its own terms was increasingly irrelevant to younger Taiwanese, who had little tangible connection to the mainland. Most people were understandably hesitant to trade the relative freedom and affluence they enjoyed in Taiwan for the uncertainties of a shotgun marriage with China.

Nor did most Taiwanese feel any great love for the KMT, whose stewardship of Taiwan had been distinguished by rampant corruption, ruthless suppression of dissent, and intolerance of local cultural traditions. Taiwan had scarcely recovered from 50 years of harsh Japanese colonial rule when Chiang's fleeing nationalist forces descended on the island in the late 1940s and launched what amounted to a campaign of cultural genocide against the Taiwanese, who over the previous 400 years had developed their own unique dialect and traditions. The Generalissimo's pogrom boiled over on 28 February 1948, when a street scuffle escalated into an island-wide purge in which an estimated 20,000 citizens were murdered by KMT goon squads, dwarfing the later death toll at Tiananmen Square. The incident was hushed up by the KMT for nearly 40 years on penalty of imprisonment or worse, but it was never forgotten by the indignant Taiwanese, whose simmering animosity toward their unwelcome KMT overlords, compounded by the ROC's precarious military standoff with mainland China, prompted Chiang Kai-Shek to impose a period of martial law that remained in effect until it was lifted in the 1980s by his son and successor, the more moderate Chiang Ching-Kuo.

By the last decade of the century, KMT veterans and their descendants made up only a fifth of the island's populace, the remainder of whom were so-called Taiwanese—progeny of Chinese migrants who predated the KMT era—plus a few hundred thousand non-Chinese derisively known as *shandiren* ("mountain people"), who are thought to have migrated to Taiwan from the Pacific islands in prehistoric times. These original inhabitants had been displaced by Chinese settlers who colonized the island following the breakup of China's Ming Dynasty in the seventeenth century.

With the end of martial law in the 1980s and the subsequent lifting of the ban on opposition parties, new political entities came into being that espoused the once-unthinkable cause of independent Taiwanese nationhood. The efforts of popularly elected representatives to force a pro-Taiwanese agenda on geriatric KMT lawmakers regularly provoked actual fistfights during parliamentary sessions, much to the amusement of the international news media. Yet despite the strong-arm tactics of veteran KMT politicians, who feared for their dream of a united motherland, and despite increasingly bellicose declarations from PRC leaders that any moves toward Taiwanese independence would be crushed with military force, opposition to KMT rule grew steadily throughout the 1990s. In Taiwan's 1992 election, opposition Democratic People's Party (DPP) candidates overcame rampant KMT intimidation, vote buying, and ballot-box stuffing to capture nearly 50 percent of the popular vote. By the end of the decade, the Taiwanese would elect their first-ever non-KMT president, in defiance of a threatening display of Chinese naval might in the Formosa Strait.

Taiwan and Mainland China were worlds apart not only politically but also culturally. Where China's disastrous Great Proletarian Cultural Revolution of 1966–76 had produced an entire generation of undereducated, emotionally scarred citizens, Taiwan's strict neo-Confucian educational system had engendered a thriving middle class of well-disciplined scholars and savvy entrepreneurs. Where Maoist zealots had wantonly destroyed countless irreplaceable cultural artifacts in the rush to bury China's feudal past, their erstwhile compatriots across the Formosa Strait took great pride in preserving their ancient heritage. And where Mao and his cronies had ruthlessly stamped out religion and "superstitious" folk practices on the mainland, Buddhism and the traditional arts continued to flourish in Taiwan.

Yet for all its emphasis on culture, and despite its people's newly won freedom of expression, I found the Taiwan of the early '90s disappointingly bereft of innovative music. Unlike China, where grinding poverty and suffocating government censorship had paradoxically given rise to a furtive but vital musical avant-garde, prosperous Taiwan had produced a generation of musicians whose creative edge had been noticeably dulled by their comfortable bourgeois lifestyle. With a few significant exceptions, Taiwanese musicians of the 1980s and early 90s seemed content to produce little else but shallow, escapist pop fare.

When Anne and I arrived, Taiwan's music scene made the slick L.A. record industry seem downright bohemian. The hottest act going was the Little Tiger Team, a sickeningly cute trio of adolescent boys that was like a Chinese version of Menudo. The island's airwaves were filled with the strains of comely starlets singing cookie-cutter hits, backed by faceless studio hacks. "Sensitive," bespectacled folksingers crooned well-worn chart-toppers like Lionel Ritchie's "Hello" ad nauseum in pricy steakhouses. And not content with afflicting the poor people of Mainland China, Richard Clayderman had blanketed Taiwan with his vapid pianism as well. Fittingly, one of his tinkly tunes was even used as the theme song for Taiwan's sanitation department, broadcast daily from badly overdriven loudspeakers mounted on the island's garbage trucks.

Thankfully, not all of Taiwan's contemporary music was this banal. Among the more compelling Taiwanese musicians of recent times was songwriter, political activist, and all-around cause célèbre Hou Dejian, the embodiment of China's post-1949 split personality. Hou had emerged from the "coffeehouse folk" movement that flowered under the relatively benign regime of Chiang Ching-Kuo in the 1970s. He was soon catapulted onto a larger stage with the release of his huge 1979 hit, "Descendants of the Dragon," a ringing statement of pan-Chinese nationalism that made Hou a lightning rod for the contentious issue of Chinese reunification.

*In the ancient East there is a dragon; China is its name.*
*In the ancient East there lives a people,*
*The dragon's heirs every one.*
*Under the claws of this mighty dragon I grew up*
*And its descendant I have become. Like it or not—*
*Once and forever, a descendant of the dragon.*

Hou grabbed headlines and reversed a trend when he defected to the mainland in 1983 to reassert his Chinese roots. Welcomed at first by a PRC government that viewed him as a useful propaganda tool, Hou became a national celebrity and important influence on the nascent rock music scene. He eventually grew disenchanted with Communist rule and in 1989 acted as a highly visible spokesperson for pro-democracy demonstrators in Tiananmen Square. The following year PRC authorities forcibly repatriated him to Taiwan, where he was arrested and briefly detained.

A handful of controversial Taiwanese rock bands such as Double X and Blacklist made waves in the 1980s, but their noisy tirades failed to catch on with audiences whose tastes ran more to Debbie Gibson and Air Supply. In a move more apropos of the PRC than Taiwan, the government even banned a Blacklist album because it contained an irreverent take-off on the ROC anthem. A few bold musicians even went so far as to advocate Taiwanese nationhood, most notably activist singer/songwriter Chen Ming-chang, who ruffled KMT feathers by singing exclusively in the Taiwanese dialect. Sadly, innovators like Chen had precious few outlets for their creative energies. I seriously doubted that there would be any place for my music either.

Following up on a job lead from Brad, Anne and I took up residence in Tainan, Taiwan's former capital and most conservative major city, renowned for its many Buddhist temples. Located at the seaward edge of the coastal plain in the island's tropical south, Tainan boasted balmy weather year-round and a much more relaxed lifestyle than frenetic Taipei. About 200 expatriate Americans, Canadians, Europeans, and Antipodeans lived in the Tainan area at the time, most of them language students at the city's National Cheng Kung University. The rest of the foreign residents were largely male slackers indulging in a sort of permanent spring break, typified by round-the-clock partying and the endless pursuit of impressionable Tainan girls.

One curious custom of the expatriate community was the

dropping of surnames in favor of more descriptive appellations. Foreigners came to be identified by the places they hailed from, as in the cases of Texas Steve, Canadian Tom, Australian Peter, and Kiwi Dave. Those with especially common names were assigned numbers, as befell the perennially confused trio of Michael 1, Michael 2, and Michael 3. Others earned their nicknames through their deeds or defining traits, notably Tofu Michael, Hippie Jim, Spaghetti Steve, and Have a Beer Michael.

Anne and I showed up in Tainan city with a single job prospect and all of US$700 between us, but we soon settled into a routine of teaching English to rich kids in the city's ubiquitous *bushibans*— private "cram schools" where college hopefuls studied math, English, music, and other subjects after regular school hours until they were fit to collapse from fatigue. I got off to a rocky start with my first teaching job, at a children's *bushiban* in the nearby countryside. The outgoing teacher had assured me that the woman who ran the school would be available to help translate and keep the students in line, but when I showed up for the first class, a neighbor explained that the schoolmistress was in the hospital because "her uncle broke her leg." Inside the classroom I found a motley assortment of kids aged 5 to 15, hell-bent on anarchy in the absence of their stern school-mistress. Objects sailed through the air, toddlers bawled, and fights broke out as I tried in vain to teach a phrase or two of English. Faced with this mayhem, I eventually abandoned the lesson plan and instead spent the next two hours playing a spirited game of keep-away with the shrieking brats. I didn't bother to show up for the following week's class.

Fortunately, classroom debacles like this were the exception. I went on to teach English to hundreds of students ranging from pre-schoolers to collegians to factory owners, forming a number of lasting friendships in the process. The money was good, the hours flexible, and my students showered me with gifts and delicacies to the point of embarrassment. Still, after the exhilaration of my musical adventures in China, the life of a foreign teacher in Tainan was decidedly anticlimactic, and I soon grew impatient to launch a fresh music project.

An opportunity arose that summer when I was introduced to Mark DeForge, a longtime expatriate who'd played bass in hardcore punk bands back in his hometown of Albany, New York, just downriver from my own hometown of Utica. Mark was something of a legend in Tainan, not least because of his impressive mastery of the Chinese language, and his English classes at the loftily named Cambridge Language Center were perennially filled to overflowing. A prolific songwriter with a subtle, razor-sharp sense of humor, a penchant for the macabre, and a gift for the deft turn of phrase, Mark was similarly chafing at musical inactivity and looking to form a band. He had already recruited Dave Matthews, a part-Maori singer and guitarist from Invercargill at the southern tip of New Zealand, and Shawn "Skip" Nagel, a drummer who'd played in a punk rock outfit named Dissent in South Dakota. With the addition of me as lead guitarist, Lost Weekend, as we called ourselves, was complete.

Named for the 1945 film that depicted a writer's grim descent into alcoholism, Lost Weekend was an unlikely mélange of musical styles and approaches, reflecting its members' widely divergent tastes and influences. The band managed to find enough common ground to produce some respectable original music, leavened with a few hip cover tunes. More importantly, Lost Weekend was allegedly the first Tainan-based band to write its own material and perform rock concerts in local pubs and other informal public venues. Up to that time, the city's handful of college rock groups had been content to play wobbly versions of Europe's "The Final Countdown" and Joan Jett's "I Hate Myself for Loving You" in the privacy of their practice rooms. (Because Taiwan is far from the established international touring circuit, any foreign rock band that took the trouble to play there instantly attained superstar status, hence the huge popularity of such unlikely artists as Jett, Lobo—authors of the cringe-inducing

"A Dog Named Boo"—and the forgettable pop clone Richard Marx, all of whom had played concerts in Taipei.)

Lost Weekend debuted at the Bushiban Pub in Taipei, a hangout for beery foreign slackers. All pumped up for our first gig in Taiwan, we traveled the 200 miles to the capital aboard one of the cut-rate "wild chicken" buses that plied the island's main north-south highway, tormented by deafening kung-fu movies shown on ceiling-mounted TVs day and night. On arriving at the Bushiban we discovered that the spaced-out American owner had failed to come up with the promised drum set and PA system. He eventually gave in to our badgering and borrowed some drums, but foolishly insisted that we use the tiny bar stereo system as our PA. Predictably, our big debut show was cut short when we blew out the miniature sound system in the middle of our second number.

The next Lost Weekend gig, arguably the first rock show ever staged in a Tainan pub, was an even bigger farce. We had persuaded a Taiwanese bar owner named Dirty Roger to let us play at his establishment one Friday night. With his six-foot-plus frame and hair cascading down to his belt, Roger was quite the standout in provincial Tainan, where he ran a series of pubs frequented largely by foreigners. On a typical night at Dirty Roger's, a couple dozen expats and their Taiwanese friends would line the bar knocking back hefty liter mugs of headache-inducing Taiwan Beer as DJ Roger spun loud classic rock on his turntables. It seemed like just the place to launch a live music scene.

Lost Weekend's show got off to a rocking start as the capacity crowd egged us on, happy to hear some live music for a change. Beer and sweat flowed freely as the night wore on. We were happily cruising through our second set when the audience suddenly fell silent. Wondering what had interrupted the merriment, we turned to see a half-dozen angry cops armed with machine guns at the side of the stage. The police barked at us to stop playing at once. The music trailed off, but poor Skip was so lost in what he was doing that he kept blissfully hammering away with his eyes closed until one of the cops yanked a cymbal stand right out from under him. The customers slunk away into the night, and a flustered Dirty Roger was soon embroiled in a heated conversation with the angry police. We assumed that there had been a noise complaint—something of an oxymoron in a city afflicted by swarms of buzzing motorbikes and other sonic assaults—but that wasn't the whole story. Roger later explained that the police were simply angry at his failure to obtain their permission to host live music, a breach of the time-honored tradition of paying off the cops up front. A wad of bills finally settled it.

Undeterred by our experience at Dirty Roger's, Lost Weekend quickly set up a second show at another foreigners' haunt, the Gemini Music Pub, where we were shoehorned onto a tiny stage adorned with floor-to-ceiling Budweiser ads. No sooner did we start playing than the cops turned up and shut us down again. The matter was again settled with a payoff, after which the police backed off from closing down future shows, including a second Lost Weekend gig at Dirty Roger's, where the well-compensated cops let us make all the racket we liked.

Lost Weekend played just a handful of shows before evaporating when various band members moved on from Tainan. Although the band was little more than a footnote in the grand scheme of things, we had succeeded in jump-starting a live music scene in Tainan that continues to this day.

After the demise of Lost Weekend I was approached by Bryce Whitwam, a keyboard player and language student from Sioux Falls, South Dakota, who had gotten the itch to play in a band again after seeing us at Dirty Roger's. Together we formed a mostly instrumental quartet successively named Trade Bill 301 (a punitive economic measure periodically leveled against the Taiwanese government in those days by the United States), the Gang of Formosa, and finally Identity Crisis, a glib comment on our multinational, polystylistic makeup.

The first edition of the band was rounded out by drummer Tom

Vest, a wickedly funny East Asian Studies major from Virginia who was learning Chinese at the university, and local bassist "Jimmy" Luo Rende, a member of one of Taiwan's aboriginal peoples. I first encountered Jimmy at one of Tainan's many faux-Western steak-houses, where he played guitar for a modest living with his wife, Nancy, a Chinese singer. Unlike the usual foppish college boys who sang weepy love songs in such establishments, Jimmy was an exceptional instrumentalist, yet modest to a fault. I was much taken with the flowing guitar improvisations he wove through the duo's other-wise banal material, and a conversation between sets led to Jimmy's eventual membership in the early Identity Crisis. After years of play-ing bland pop songs on the restaurant circuit, it must have been a strange yet liberating experience to play everything from Japanese movie soundtracks to art-rock with a band of foreign transients. Sadly, my friendship with Jimmy was also a window on the racism endured by Taiwan's ethnic minorities, whose gift for music affords one of the few possible escape routes from a life of dead-end poverty and alcoholism.

A total of 10 players passed through Identity Crisis over its year-long lifespan, with a core lineup of me, Bryce, Tom, and the impressive bassist Andreas Vath, a language student from Munich. Other important contributors included multi-instrumentalist Volk-er Wiedersheim, who went on to become music editor of the major German newspaper *Hannover Zeitung*, and French violist Fréderic Eymard, an accomplished classical player who experienced a jazz epiphany while guesting with Identity Crisis. Disappointingly, the band only managed to recruit one Taiwanese player, the superb drummer "Spike" Tsao Hsin, formerly of island-wide battle-of-the-bands champions Metal Fon (sic). It was never clear whether the local musicians' disinterest in playing with us was due to differences of musical taste or discomfort with the cultural distance between us. Probably both.

To our surprise, Identity Crisis evolved into a genuinely interest-ing and unusually eclectic musical entity unlike any other group we had yet heard in Taiwan. The band developed a sizable repertoire of original instrumental pieces encompassing jazz, progressive rock, film music, adapted Chinese traditional tunes, and even a twisted reggae version of Richard Clayderman's garbage truck theme song. Identity Crisis played roughly 30 shows over the winter of 1990-91 at pubs, steakhouses, and college events, including a university gala where we played beneath a huge scarlet-and-gold banner proclaiming "Youth Gone Wild." Some of our most memorable gigs took place at nontraditional venues that only underscored the absurdity of our cultural displacement. It was exceedingly strange playing wacky Identity Crisis originals like "Pock Market" and "The Heimlich Maneuver" in such unusual contexts as the venerable Lu Erh Men temple, where we performed as part of Taoist holiday festivities, or on the front steps of the newly opened Liang Mei Department Store among throngs of bewildered shoppers.

Our musical activities were greatly facilitated by the ready availability of high-quality musical equipment in Tainan, which boasted a half-dozen music shops offering an impressive selection of state-of-the-art instruments and sound systems both for sale and for rent. In fact, there would have been no bands otherwise, for among the expatriate musicians, only Andreas and I possessed our own instruments at first. I was greatly relieved that I no longer had to rely on the type of jerry-built, temperamental sound gear I'd been forced to use in China, and my sonic palette expanded considerably as a result. Identity Crisis and other foreign musicians formed a symbiotic relationship with a friendly music store owner named Mr. Ou, who rented us fully equipped rehearsal rooms for the ridiculously low fee of US$4 per hour and supplied drums, amplifiers, and PA systems for our gigs at incredibly cheap rates. In return, the foreign bands gave Mr. Ou face by taking part in many of the musical events he organized throughout the city.

One such gig was at the grand opening of a Sichuanese restaurant in the small town of Chiali, some miles outside of Tainan. The owner had seen us play at the department store and thought a foreign band would lend some cachet to his restaurant's debut. He contacted us through Mr. Ou and offered to pay us handsomely as well as provide equipment and dinner. We showed up at the appointed time and discovered that we would not be playing inside the restaurant, as expected, but outside on the sidewalk, where the equipment was already set up—facing a busy arterial. As the oblivious patrons chowed down on sumptuous Sichuanese dishes on the other side of the glass, the band serenaded a nonstop stream of whizzing motorcycles and belching trucks. Not one person stopped to listen. Afterwards, a lackey took us to a distant hot-pot restaurant and sat silent as we ate; apparently the restaurateur didn't want a bunch of scruffy foreign musicians mingling with his guests.

Identity Crisis gained a small but appreciative following among expatriates and local musicians, but the Tainan public didn't really know what to make of our split musical personality. As it turned out, we found a far more appreciative audience when we received an unexpected invitation to tour China.

For the past year I had been scheming to set up a concert tour of Mainland China for a band that would include musicians I'd played with in Seattle. The plan had been gestating since early 1990, when a member of Zhang Xing's entourage had raised the possibility of my touring Chinese cities with support from his management company. My previous success performing in China had shown me that with the right contacts, a multi-city tour by a Western band might be more feasible than I'd initially imagined. The prospect was irresistible, for to the best of my knowledge no Western group had yet toured China without explicit government sponsorship, much less playing the type of music I envisioned. Touring with like-minded players would also enable me to present more fully realized music without the limitations of performing solo or with inexperienced Chinese players, as I had in Chengdu. A serendipitous confluence of happenstance and design had brought me the opportunity to introduce thousands, perhaps millions, of curious Chinese listeners to a novel musical experience. I wanted to do it the right way, with excellent musicians and solid, innovative material.

Not long after I'd settled in Taiwan, I contacted my chosen musicians in Seattle and floated the tour proposal. It wasn't hard to get them on board—after all, it isn't every day that a musician is offered a chance to tour an exotic communist country—but making the dream a reality wasn't quite so simple. Confident that I could assemble a first-rate band, I tried to reach Zhang Xing's associate in Shanghai and tell him we were available for the tour he'd so confidently sketched out a year earlier. But now that I'd raised my Seattle friends' hopes, the Shanghai connection wasn't returning my calls. I was just about to abandon the plan when my former manager in Chengdu, Tang Lei, telephoned out of the blue with news that Chinese rock legend Cui Jian had listened to my *Shadow in Dreams* and was encouraging me to play in Beijing. Here was the breakthrough I'd been hoping for, with a chance to meet and perhaps even play with China's most important rock musician in the bargain! However, one serious hitch remained: The band would have to cover its own travel expenses to Beijing. For me, traveling from Taiwan to Beijing was relatively cheap and well worth the sacrifice, but for my prospective bandmates, flying from Seattle to China could easily cost US$1,000 per person, so they regretfully declined.

Despite this setback, I was loath to let the opportunity slip, since there was no guarantee of a similar offer in the future. If the Americans couldn't afford to fly to Beijing, well, there was always Identity Crisis. Sure, we were complete unknowns in China, but who wasn't? Besides, we had the advantage of being based in nearby Taiwan and having a fair amount of experience with Chinese culture and language between us. Satisfied that the band was more than capable of pulling off the gig, I asked Andreas, Bryce, and Tom if they were up for the tour. Not surprisingly, they were all eager to make the trip and willing to pay their own way, so I contacted Tang Lei to confirm that we were coming. After a month of intensive rehearsals, Identity Crisis was off to Beijing to rendezvous with Cui Jian.

# CHAPTER 13

# Cui Jian

In post-Mao China, Cui Jian was Bob Dylan, John Lennon, and Kurt Cobain all rolled into one, a one-man rock-and-roll revolution whose moving songs of alienation spoke volumes to a generation searching for meaning in a rapidly changing and increasingly globalized China. As the reluctant spokesperson for China's disenfranchised youth, Cui Jian will forever be linked in the public's mind to the democracy movement that was crushed by the tanks at Tiananmen. The image of the rocker defiantly rallying hunger strikers with his stirring outsider anthems epitomized a generation's struggles and aspirations.

I first became aware of Cui Jian in Chengdu during the summer of 1989, when my teenage hipster friend Xiao Fei loaned me his copy of the singer's breakout album *Rock and Roll on the New Long March*. Though my guitar students had been raving about the rocker for some time, I hadn't given their recommendations much credence, for most of the Chinese bands I'd heard up to that time were disappointingly lightweight. But the moment I first heard Cui Jian's music I became an instant fan. His songs possessed an undeniable *gravitas* that made a mockery of the flaccid pop tunes of the day, and the musicianship was top-notch and thoroughly contemporary. I bought my own copy of *Rock and Roll on the New Long March* and soon wore it out on the borrowed boom box in our apartment.

Born in 1961 to musically inclined parents of ethnic Korean descent, Cui Jian revealed an early gift for music and by age 20 had already landed a job playing trumpet with the prestigious Beijing Philharmonic Orchestra. Most Chinese musicians would have given their eyeteeth for such an opportunity, with its promise of stable lifetime employment, but by this time Cui Jian had already been smitten by the rock and roll he was hearing on tapes spirited into the country by Western tourists and students. Initially inspired by the likes of Simon and Garfunkel and the rough-hewn "Northwest Wind" genre of contemporary Chinese folk music, he learned to play guitar and started singing in public, at first covering tunes by well-known singers and then eventually writing his own material.

Much like Zhang Xing, the young Cui Jian first attracted widespread attention with an appearance on a TV talent contest, in 1985. His impact on viewers was similar to that of Elvis Presley as he gyrated on the *Ed Sullivan Show* in 1950s America. Even at this early stage in his career, Cui Jian's songs showed a preoccupation with weightier issues than the usual gauzy romantic fantasies, dealing with such sensitive topics as individualism, sexuality, blind adherence to tradition, and, by inference, the integrity of the Chinese Communist Party. To a generation numbed by propaganda, the honesty and realism of Cui Jian's lyrics was a clarion call. Equally important, his tunes rocked with an authenticity that earlier Chinese musicians had never fully internalized.

Before long young people all over China were banging out their hero's tunes on beat-up guitars in campus dormitories and coffeehouses. All too predictably, the rebel rocker's growing popularity set him on a collision course with the Chinese government, who painted him as a bad element. He was expelled from the Beijing Philharmonic Orchestra and soon afterward was forbidden to perform in public for a year after angering a highly placed military official with his irreverent rendition of the hallowed revolutionary paean "Nanniwan" ("South Muddy Bay"). What scandalized his detractors was not the song's lyrics, which were exactly the same as the patriotic original, but the way in which they were framed by 'barbarian' music; authorities are always deeply offended when an artist like Cui Jian has the insolence to appropriate and thus debase such sacred political emblems by situating them within a foreign musical context.

Where Zhang Xing represented the attainment of a fairy-tale wealth and glamour unimaginable to generations of Chinese accustomed to drabness and privation, Cui Jian couldn't have been more different. With his deliberately scruffy appearance and rough, untrained voice, he personified an emerging generation of alienated urban youth. Frustrated by lack of opportunity and weary of the Communist Party's increasingly bankrupt ideology, Cui Jian and his peers eschewed the glossy escapism of Zhang Xing and his ilk in favor of a gritty urban realism.

After an early stint with the cover band Seven Ply Board, Cui Jian started honing his own material in ADO, an innovative Beijing band that included the phenomenal drummer Zhong Yongguang ("Sar") and two renegade foreign embassy employees, Hungarian bassist Kassai Balasz and Madagascan guitarist Eddie Randriama Pionona. Ever since China launched its own version of *glasnost* under paramount leader Deng Xiaoping, these and other foreign players had been introducing Beijing musicians to the wonders of reggae, blues, and jazz, and their participation brought a rhythmic dynamism to Cui Jian's tunes that lifted them above mere folk songs. With ADO, Cui Jian released his 1986 opus *Rock and Roll on the New Long March*, soon to become the defining statement of China's new lost generation. A solid collection of original tunes, the album raised the bar for all future Chinese rock music and provided a potent and timely anthem in Cui Jian's most enduringly beloved song, "Yi Wu Suo You" ("Nothing to My Name").

## Yi Wu Suo You

*How long have I been asking you,*
*When will you come with me?*

*But you always laugh at me,*
*For I have nothing to my name.*

*I want to give you my hope.*
*I want to help make you free.*
*But you always laugh at me,*
*For I have nothing to my name.*

*Oh, oh... when will you come with me?*
*Oh, oh... when will you come with me?*

*The earth is turning under your feet.*
*The waters of life are flowing free.*
*But you always laugh at me,*
*For I have nothing to my name.*

*Why do you laugh at the pack on my back?*
*Why do I always keep on going?*
*The old horse stands before you,*
*With nothing to my name.*

*Oh, oh... when will you come with me?*
*Oh, oh... when will you come with me?*

*I tell you I've been waiting a long time,*
*I tell you, here's my final plea:*
*I want to grab you by the hands*
*And take you away with me.*

*Your hands, they are trembling.*
*Your eyes, they overflow with tears.*
*Do you really mean to tell me,*
*You love me as I am?*

*Oh, oh... when will you come with me?*
*Oh, oh... then you will come with me.*

"Yi Wu Suo You" resonated deeply with a youth culture grasping for meaning in a China afflicted by institutionalized corruption, rampant materialism, widening social stratification, and an increasingly out-of-touch socialist ideology. Like Dylan, Woody Guthrie, and a handful of others, Cui Jian managed to distill a generation's fears and longings into a simple four-minute song. It's no wonder that "Yi Wu Suo You" was spontaneously adopted as the unofficial anthem of the demonstrators at Tiananmen Square.

Yet while he is perpetually identified with the 1989 student movement, Cui Jian's involvement was in fact limited to a single concert with ADO in Tiananmen Square. The singer's reputation as a rebel is deceptive, for he has always taken great pains to avoid making direct political statements in his songs, instead employing suggestive imagery and innuendo that can be interpreted in numerous ways. A prime example is his early 1990s tune "The Last Shot," a mournful ballad written from the perspective of a dying soldier and peppered with recorded gunshots all too reminiscent of Tiananmen. When asked if the song referred to the events of June 4, he insisted that it was about the 1979 Sino-Vietnamese border clash, neatly shifting the subject from protest to patriotism, though of course the song can be construed either way. In China, what's important is not necessarily what's said, but what is *not* said.

Cui Jian has doggedly resisted discussing politics and maintains that his songs are concerned only with universal human issues. He has also complained that foreign journalists only increase his woes by trying to politicize his music. In a sense, given his refusal to unequivocally criticize authority, Cui Jian could be viewed as a consummate performance artist, enjoying all the notoriety of a political subversive without ever having leveled a substantive critique of his country's policies. Although viewed by many as the epitome of the rebel archetype, Cui Jian's customary ambiguity places him within a longstanding Chinese tradition that privileges circumspection and obliquity over confrontation.

And what of Cui Jian's music? Apart from the Mandarin lyrics and occasional use of traditional instruments for coloristic effect, his songs tend to borrow heavily from Western rock, pop, and funk precedents. In his early work, the influence of Bob Marley, the Police, Talking Heads, and other music then circulating in Beijing's foreign community is evident, and the contributions of foreign collaborators Eddie and Balasz loom large. In fact, many Western listeners are disappointed to find that Cui Jian's music is not as "Chinese" as they'd expected. It can be argued that his most distinctive songs are those that do incorporate Chinese elements such as the *dizi* (bamboo flute) and *guzheng* (an ancient zither). But Cui Jian doesn't want his music to be pinned down to a narrow cultural continuum, preferring to view his work in the context of a worldwide rock-and-roll insurgency. The best of his songs genuinely *rock*, and unlike many Chinese rock musicians who followed in his wake, he has continued to grow and experiment musically into the twenty-first century.

Cui Jian escaped serious punishment in the aftermath of Tiananmen, presumably to avoid setting off a generational backlash. But like most of his peers in China's contemporary arts scene, he was forced to keep a low profile in the wake of the government's crackdown on dissidents, and he found even fewer opportunities to perform than before June 4.

The following year Cui Jian made a canny proposition to the government: If he was allowed to undertake a national concert tour, he would donate all profits to the upcoming Asian Games, to be held in Beijing. It was no secret that Deng's beleaguered regime viewed the Asian Games as an opportunity to restore its tarnished international image after the Tiananmen disgrace. Cui Jian's request was granted, and he set off on a "New Long March" tour that took him to arenas throughout the country. Enormous crowds attended his concerts and responded with a passion that alarmed authorities, dancing in the aisles and provocatively flashing "V for Victory" signs. It was on

*Cui Jian in concert, Zhuhai 1991 (Spike Mafford)*

this tour that Cui Jian first made what is perhaps his most overtly political statement by wearing a bright red blindfold over his eyes while performing his song "A Piece of Red Cloth." While the song's lyrics remained characteristically ambiguous, the symbolism of the visual gesture was unmistakable. Fearing an outbreak of public disorder, officials in Beijing abruptly canceled the singer's remaining dates after an especially rousing concert in Chengdu, which was still recovering from its own bloody crackdown in June 1989. Cui Jian's road trip was nonetheless highly significant, as it inspired the formation of dozens of grassroots rock bands in China's hinterlands.

For the next few years Cui Jian was restricted to playing surreptitious gigs at private gatherings in Beijing. He was expressly banned from any university campus, and his notoriety made large-scale public concerts out of the question. The 1991 release of his second album, *Solution*, did little to improve relations with the authorities, containing as it did both the sacrilegious "Nanniwan" and the provocative "Last Shot." It would be several years before the PRC government allowed him to resume touring, by which time the Chinese public was more bent on making money than on fomenting revolution.

Just after Cui Jian's aborted 1990 concert tour, Tang Lei sent him a copy of my *Shadow in Dreams* through a mutual friend in Beijing. Intrigued by what he heard and by what I had managed to accomplish in provincial Chengdu, Cui Jian encouraged Tang Lei to invite me to the Chinese capital for some underground concerts with my band. Needless to say, I jumped on this remarkable opportunity without a moment's hesitation.

# CHAPTER 14

# IDENTITY CRISIS IN BEIJING

In early April 1991, Identity Crisis traveled to China to meet with Cui Jian and embark on an underground concert tour. We had initially planned to travel by air to Beijing via Hong Kong, but so many Taiwanese were visiting their ancestral villages on the mainland for the annual Tomb-Sweeping holiday that we found it impossible to procure airline tickets. Instead, we made a circuitous three-day journey to Beijing that involved a 25-hour steamship passage from Taiwan to the then Portuguese colony of Macau on the south China coast, an overnight ferry ride up the Pearl River to the city of Guangzhou (better known in the West as Canton), and finally a China Airlines flight to Beijing. Accompanying us was our good friend Andy Clarke, an expatriate New Yorker living in Tainan who decided to tag along to buoy our *esprit de corps*. When boarding the SS *Macmosa* ("Macau-Formosa") in the Taiwanese port city of Kaohsiung, we were delighted to bump into another expat friend, Peter Shotwell, who was en route to southern China on a business trip. An inveterate vagabond with a wealth of extraordinary traveler's tales, Peter knew a good adventure when he smelled one and soon abandoned his own plans in favor of traveling with us to Beijing.

Upon arriving in the Chinese capital we were informed that the band was scheduled to play a concert in a matter of hours. Worn out from three days of travel with our bulky equipment, we scarcely had time to react to this news before Cui Jian himself showed up at our hotel to treat us to the requisite Peking duck dinner. We took an immediately liking to the modest and thoughtful musician. Soft-spoken and genuinely interested in our unknown band, he would never have been taken for a superstar were it not for the throng of autograph seekers that instantly beset him in the hotel lobby.

After dinner our hosts took us to the unlikely venue for the night's performance, Pierre Cardin's trendy, upscale restaurant Maxim's, one of the first beachheads of Euro decadence in China. Somewhat insulated on account of its international ownership, Maxim's was a sort of gray zone where fringe activities like rock concerts were more or less tolerated by the Public Security Bureau; many consider the venue to have been the cradle of the budding Beijing rock music scene. The hefty cover charge for events (a steep 30 RMB when we played) was an effective deterrent to attendance by average citizens, so the "parties" (a euphemism for rock shows) were patronized large-ly by foreigners and the privileged children of Communist Party officials—not exactly the type of audience we'd anticipated when preparing for our trip back in Tainan.

To our surprise, the stage in the restaurant's back room boasted an expensive, state-of-the-art sound system that was far better than the rigs I was accustomed to dealing with in the U.S., much less Chengdu. But we were not so pleased to learn that two other foreign bands were also booked to play that night, robbing our "pioneer-ing" cross-cultural expedition of some of its luster. Watching these American students and businessmen crank out tired roadhouse rock for an audience of bobbing blond heads, I figured we might as well be playing in New Jersey—had we traveled all the way to Beijing just to share the stage with a bunch of preening expats?

Our entire tour nearly collapsed right then and there when the keyboardist for one of the supporting bands helped himself to our digital synthesizer without bothering to ask for permission. Unaware that the instrument required a foreign voltage converter, he plugged its 110-volt power cable directly into a 220-volt electrical outlet; soon smoke was actually issuing from between the keys. Convinced that this bozo had fried an expensive instrument that was essential to our tour—and which we had rented from the sympathetic music shop owner Mr. Ou in Taiwan—I became so agitated that I had to leave the building and walk around the block to regain my composure. To my immense relief, I returned to find that the keyboard had somehow miraculously repaired itself; otherwise, we would have had to return directly to Taiwan owing Mr. Ou several thousand dollars.

Hours later we finally took the stage, cranky with fatigue. Most of the foreigners retreated to the bar in the adjacent room, indifferent to us, but the void was soon filled by a large number of Beijing musicians and music fans that we hadn't seen earlier in the evening. Cui Jian and his associates had apparently spread word of our show throughout the music community, and the musicians, bored as we were with the opening bands' sophomoric stage antics and stale pub-rock tunes, had been waiting outside all this time for us to begin.

What followed was one of the most memorable gigs of my life. Forgetting our weariness and disorientation, Identity Crisis rose to the occasion and delivered one of our best shows ever, stimulated by the palpable enthusiasm of the crowd, who pressed in at the front of the stage and egged us on with shouts of approval. Now this was more like it!

Following the same approach that had worked so well for me in Chengdu, the band played a set that was eclectic in the extreme, spanning funk, hard rock, jazz ballads, the theme from the 1987 film *The Last Emperor*, adapted Chinese folk music, and even a

IDENTITY CRISIS
自我放逐

THE 1991 CHINA TOUR
一九九一年中國巡迴表演

sinister heavy metal dirge. We had also learned several of Cui Jian's songs in the hope that he'd sing one with us. Toward the end of our set we took a deep breath and invited him to join us. After some initial hesitation—either he was loath to draw heat from the authorities, or he didn't trust us to play his songs right—he was literally pushed on stage by the excited audience. Beijing's rock icon strapped on a borrowed guitar as we played the opening chords of his classic "Yi Wu Suo You" and soon joined in, sounding a bit rusty at first but growing more relaxed as he realized that we'd actually done our homework. By the end of the tune the animated singer was clearly in his element, grinning and belting out his stirring lyrics with gusto. He had an uncanny effect on the crowd, who remained on their feet cheering, singing along, and swaying back and forth with hands held aloft. The synergy between audience and performer was the strongest I'd ever felt, a powerful affirmation of Cui Jian's impact on China's young people. I was deeply moved and proud that Identity Crisis had done his song justice. The show concluded with an equally strong version of another favorite from *Rock and Roll on the New Long March*, "Chu Zou" ("Stepping Out"). Afterward an international hotel manager who kept a close eye on the Beijing rock scene characterized the event as "magic."

Two days later Identity Crisis sat in with Yinhuochong—the band I'd toured with in Sichuan—at the glitzy Taiwan Hotel, to the puzzlement of the establishment's well-heeled clientele. The next afternoon we had a cultural experience of an altogether different kind when Yinhuochong treated us to an extravagant lunch at one of their favorite restaurants. At the band's urging, the chef served up course after savory course, beaming with pride when we praised his culinary skills. Toward the end of the meal he brought out a plate of what looked like beef stir-fried with green peppers and insisted that we try this "delicious local specialty." I sampled the dish and found the meat a bit tough and chewy, its nondescript flavor masked by a rich sauce. Hovering over our table, the chef asked how I liked the dish. I politely replied that it was tasty indeed. With a mischievous glint in his eye, he then asked me to guess what kind of meat it was. I ventured beef, at which he shook his head vigorously and broke into loud guffaws. My next guess, pork, elicited still more merriment. I could tell from its texture that the meat wasn't poultry or rabbit, and realized that my choices were rapidly narrowing. With a sinking feeling, I asked if it was dog meat. "Yes!" the chef hissed triumphantly. "I know you foreigners don't like to eat dogs! Hahahahaha!!!" I cleaned my plate just to spite him.

Over the next 10 days Identity Crisis played several more public and private shows in Beijing. A series of informal jam sessions took place at Cui Jian's private rehearsal studio, attended by members of ADO, the excellent pianist Liang Heping, unhinged punk rocker He Yong, and other Beijing rock musicians. Many of the friendships forged at these convivial get-togethers would continue for years. One afternoon Tom Vest and I accepted an invitation to check out a rehearsal by Hei Bao ("Black Panther"), who would soon become one of China's most commercially successful rock bands. It wasn't hard to see why the band had achieved such success—in stark contrast to their impoverished peers, Hei Bao were the beneficiaries of tens of thousands of dollars' worth of professional sound equipment donated by wealthy patrons in Taiwan. And while most Beijing musicians were forced to rehearse in their bedrooms, Hei Bao had the run of a huge gymnasium built for the Asian Games, complete with stage lighting and a sophisticated concert PA system.

Later that week Cui Jian's manager, Liang Weiping, brought us to the Citli All-Night Club, a disco he'd rented for a "musical exchange" between Identity Crisis and local musicians. We walked into the club expecting a relaxed, low-key jam session, only to discover more than 100 Beijing musicians, artists, and filmmakers waiting for us to give a concert. Under intense scrutiny we delivered a respectable set, followed by various Beijing rock groups, ad-hoc jam sessions, and the first reunion of Cui Jian with his former band, ADO, in more than two years. The event was captured on videotape by Beijing Film Studio director Ning Ying, who'd worked on the production of Bernardo Bertolucci's *The Last Emperor*.

It was here that I first realized the surprising extent of Beijing's underground music community. Despite existing right under the nose of the central government, the capital's rock-and-roll subculture was far more daring than that of any other Chinese city. By the early 1990s dozens of bands had emerged whose music deliberately flew in the face of the status quo. What their music lacked in finesse it more than made up for in passion, possessing an ardor and immediacy that were largely absent in the music of Taiwan and Hong Kong, the bastions of "free" China. But the rockers' rebellion came at a steep price. Rock concerts had been virtually outlawed by the government, which viewed rock music as an agent of moral decay, and when shows did take place, they were invariably shut down by armed police.

The government blamed the emergence of Chinese rock on pernicious Western influence, and to a large degree they were right. Deng Xiaoping's open-door policy had precipitated a steady influx of foreign music and entertainers, inadvertently jump-starting the Chinese rock phenomenon, or "Chinarock," as it later came to be known. The first major international rock concert in China, by British New Wave rock group Wham! in 1985, spawned an entire generation of wannabe rockers and, in time-honored tradition, left their parents scandalized by singer George Michael's salacious stage antics. The emergent rock scene was enthusiastically nurtured by Beijing's sizable expatriate community, who gave budding rockers their first opportunities to strut their stuff at semiprivate parties held at embassies and foreign-run establishments like Maxim's. The importance of these parties in fostering the nascent rock movement cannot be overstated.

Despite—or perhaps because of—government suppression of rock and roll, a vital underground music community took root in Beijing that had obvious parallels in the beatniks and hippies of post-WWII America and London's punk movement of the late 1970s. Like their British and American counterparts, Chinese rockers flaunted social conventions by growing out their hair, wearing black leather, smoking hashish, and espousing free love. But where Occidental rockers enjoyed plentiful performance opportunities and broad media exposure, Beijing rock musicians operated largely in obscurity and on dangerously thin political ice. Denied access to a wider audience by a hostile government, Beijing rockers found sympathetic listeners in the city's art, literary, and filmmaking circles. And as the bands grew more experienced, they became increasingly adept at outfoxing the authorities, organizing word-of-mouth concerts at makeshift performance spaces throughout the city, much like the rave culture that would emerge in urban centers of the West later in the decade.

Ironically, in the 1990s, communist China was one of the few places left in the world where rock and roll was still vital and transformative. While rock music in the West had been absorbed into the very establishment it originally reacted against, the fledgling Chinese rock scene still existed for the most part at the margins of what was artistically and socially acceptable in a still nominally communist society. At its best, the music distilled the essence of what rock and roll was initially all about: self-determination, sexual liberation, questioning of authority and tradition. The best Chinese rock still had an aura of danger and ecstatic release that is difficult to imagine in contemporary America, where the freedom to make noise and thumb one's nose at the establishment was taken for granted.

What I found especially remarkable about China's pioneer rockers, apart from the fact that they existed at all in such an inhospitable environment, was the sense of solidarity that characterized the community. Allowing for the inevitable factional rivalries that we were not privy to, there seemed to be more cooperation and less cutthroat competition than I'd observed in other music scenes. The early Chinese rockers shared equipment, rehearsal spaces, and the few available gigs, and they supported each other regardless of stylistic differences, united by the common experience of being outsiders participating in a social experiment that carried far graver risks than those faced by musicians in the West. I wondered if these values would survive China's inexorable metamorphosis into a Western-style market economy, where self-interest rules the day.

Among the groups active in Beijing at the time of our visit were Self-Education, a gloomy, alienated New Wave band in the tradition of Joy Division; hard rockers the Yellow Race and the provocatively named 1989; rising metal stars Tang Dynasty; and the aforementioned arena-rock outfit Hei Bao. Perhaps the most radical figure of all was He Yong, widely considered China's first punk rocker. A charter member of the Beijing rock fraternity, He Yong gained notoriety in 1989 when he played for the protesters in Tiananmen Square with his group Mayday. His most controversial song, "Garbage Dump," is a furious indictment of China's deepening environmental, social, and spiritual decay. With its splintered, dissonant piano slashings and He Yong's howls of indignation joined to a driving rock pulse, "Garbage Dump" ranks among the most militant statements of Chinese rock:

> *The place where we live is like a garbage dump*
> *We're all insects fighting and squabbling*
> *We eat our conscience and shit out our thoughts*
> *Is there anything we can do? No—tear it down!*

While the early Beijing rock and roll scene was admirably communitarian in most respects, it was even more male dominated than its Western counterpart. Fortunately, a small number of women players had begun to make inroads on the boys' club. In 1989, five female instrumentalists with backgrounds in state traditional music troupes formed Cobra, China's first all-woman rock band. Adopting a retro aesthetic rooted in 1950s American rock and roll, the band persevered in the face of skepticism and condescension from male rockers to build a successful career that continued well into the 1990s, including several international tours. Another important figure in the women's rock movement was Weihua, a former English-language newscaster for China Central TV. After the station silenced her for publicly criticizing the government's actions at Tiananmen, Weihua quit her post to begin a new career as singer for Breathing, a band that made a splash on the Beijing scene in the early 1990s. Weihua attended the Identity Crisis show at Maxim's, and some of us played with members of Cobra during our stay, jamming loosely on Chuck Berry–style numbers sung in Mandarin.

Hoping to reach audiences that couldn't afford the astronomical cover charges at clubs like Maxim's, Identity Crisis also tried to arrange shows at Beijing universities. Having taught English at a Beijing technical university in 1988, Bryce telephoned a contact in the school's foreign affairs office to ask if we could give a concert there. With the Tiananmen incident still festering, we wagered that our chances of performing for college students were slim indeed, but to our surprise school officials gave us the thumbs-up. Bryce went to the university to settle the details with the director of foreign affairs and the student body president. Meanwhile, news arrived that some of Bryce's former students had arranged shows for us at nearby Beijing and Qinghua universities. We could hardly believe our luck.

Two days later, Bryce received word that all three university shows had been called off. It seemed that higher-ranking officials at the institutions had caught wind of what was afoot and had instantly canceled our concerts. Officially, the explanation given by the technical university was that the auditorium was reserved for use by a dance club, but the real reason was clearly the general clampdown on student gatherings following the Tiananmen debacle. It's likely that our association with Cui Jian weighed heavily against us, for we'd been forewarned that he would be barred from any university campus to prevent him from joining us on stage. (Word of our Maxim's collaboration had traveled quickly throughout the city.) The fiasco taught us that dealing openly with government officials was a sure route to failure. Cui Jian and his friends had been skeptical about the university shows from the start, as they had learned through bitter experience that one must resort to stealth in order to play "yellow" (decadent, in Chinese parlance) music in Beijing.

Not all of our activities in Beijing were musical. Though I never managed to visit the Great Wall, some of us did get to explore the Forbidden City—on LSD, no less. The psychedelics definitely enhanced the spectacular architecture and artworks, but the throngs of tourists no doubt wondered what was prompting our uncontrollable gusts of laughter.

Later the same day, we were fortunate to visit Peter Shotwell's friend Sol Adler, a legendary foreign resident of China who had personally known Mao and other pivotal figures in modern Chinese history. A British national, Adler had been in the employ of the U.S. government as an economic adviser to Generalissimo Chiang Kai-Shek in China's temporary wartime capital of Chongqing during the late 1930s and early 1940s. Although Adler moved among the inner circles of the KMT and even played bridge with the Generalissimo and notorious dragon lady Madame Soong, his sympathies lay with the Chinese communists, who had formed an uneasy wartime coalition with their mortal enemies the KMT in order to better resist the Japanese military's inexorable advance into the Chinese heartland. In Chongqing, Adler befriended communist leader Zhou En-Lai, who later rewarded him with honorary citizenship in the newly established People's Republic of China, an honor conferred on only a handful of foreigners. In return, Adler advised the newly formed government on global economic affairs. It was a great privilege to receive a firsthand history lesson from the elderly Adler in the attractive surroundings of his spacious Beijing courtyard dwelling, which had once belonged to top military man Lin Biao, Mao's onetime second-in-command and would-be assassin.

Our final show in Beijing took place at another odd venue, this time a converted movie theater with a 360-degree panoramic screen. Identity Crisis headlined a bill that also included Cobra, the newly reactivated ADO, and various guest musicians. Wary of possible harassment from the Public Security Bureau, the theater manager had agreed to stage the concert only on the condition that Cui Jian not perform. His caution was well founded, as about 40 uniformed police—roughly one cop for every 10 audience members—stood by throughout the show.

The evening passed without incident until Cui Jian surprised everyone by joining Cobra on stage for a version of his song "Chu Zou." A thrill rippled through the crowd—was the bad boy of Chinese rock going to defy orders and sing after all? The police quickly snapped to attention, but the embattled rocker merely raised his trumpet to his lips and provided understated accompaniment to Cobra singer Wang Rui Fang. Satisfied that no political outburst was imminent, the cops went back to looking bored. Later in the song, Cui Jian suddenly leaned toward the microphone with a mischievous grin and made as if he was going to sing, but merely added innocuous wordless harmonies. Even this was enough to elicit loud, spontaneous cheers from the audience. After this little cat-and-mouse game, Cui Jian left the stage and the security forces relaxed again.

The high point of the concert was a jam session featuring members of Identity Crisis and ADO, abetted by Cui Jian on trumpet, American music promoter Kenny Bloom on saxophone, and the inventive Liang Heping on keyboards. We played a blues, Liang Heping's jazz arrangement of the traditional Chinese shepherd's song "Mu Yang Qu," and my old workhorse "Hot Pot." The audience, a mixed assemblage of Beijing hipsters and trendy expats, bopped along energetically. At the night's close a defiant Cui Jian finally went for broke and sang a gripping solo interpretation of the infamous "Nanniwan." The cops stiffened as the aroused audience crowded close to the stage, but fortunately the unauthorized performance passed without further incident.

# CHAPTER 15

# BANISHED SOULS

Moving on from Beijing, Identity Crisis made the two-day train journey to my former home of Chengdu, following the Yellow and Wei river valleys westward into China's ancestral heartland before angling south across Sichuan to the provincial capital. Since we hadn't secured any firm commitments, this leg of the tour was a bit of a gamble, but I managed to parlay my reputation as a minor local celebrity into five sizable university concerts (including two shows at my alma mater, Chengdu University of Science & Technology) in addition to lesser gigs at the Flying Eagle Beer Pub and the tiny Liu Xiao bar, where the entire band played through a single 10-inch practice amp.

In contrast to repressed Beijing, where all our attempts to play large public shows had come to naught, we met with surprisingly little opposition from university officials in Chengdu. The one exception was Sichuan Music Conservatory, where even my status as a former guest lecturer couldn't prevent the cancellation of a sixth engagement by school authorities scandalized at the news that we'd played with Cui Jian in Beijing.

Even my previous experiences playing in Chengdu didn't prepare me for the overwhelming audience response to the Identity Crisis shows. Thousands of young people turned out to see the first Western band to play in the isolated Sichuanese capital, and hundreds more were turned away. Students at one of our two sold-out concerts at Western Medical University shattered a glass door trying to force their way into the hall, while others climbed in through second-floor windows. At one show, an audience member drummed on a desktop so zealously with his fists that he actually broke his hand—and later insisted that it had been worth it! Students made huge posters and banners and presented us with photographs and gifts. We also made a great excuse for the concert organizers to eat and drink beyond their means.

Unlike Beijing, where Cui Jian and his circle had the wherewithal to rent or borrow professional equipment for their underground concerts, facilities in Chengdu remained crude at best. We were traveling light and hence couldn't carry bulky items like amplifiers and a drum set around with us, so we had to make do with whatever equipment was at hand. Now and then we were lucky enough to scrounge satisfactory gear from local shops. More often we had to settle for shoddy drums, buzzing amps, and no PA system at all.

The biggest show of the entire tour took place in a vast outdoor amphitheater at Chengdu Electrical University. Comically, the organizers were officers of the campus branch of the Communist Youth League who professed a fervent love of rock and roll. By now we knew better than to count on getting adequate equipment, so we made the communist rockers promise that they would furnish proper instrument amplifiers.

When our hosts came to collect us on the day of the gig, we anxiously inquired about the amps and were told that we would have use of "a very good amplifier—very big!" Just one? Sure enough, we arrived at the concert venue to find nothing but a stadium-size PA system. We would have no choice but to plug all of our instruments directly into the oversized PA and pray that everything would sound okay.

With show time fast approaching, we hurriedly set up our equipment in the hope that we would get a decent sound check for a change, but no sooner did we unpack our instruments than the organizers announced that it was time to leave for dinner. We politely declined, explaining that we would rather get our sound squared away than eat just then, but the Communist Youth League had given these penniless students money to buy us dinner, and they were not about to forfeit the opportunity to gorge themselves in our honor. Brushing off all practical considerations, our hosts ordered us into a minibus and drove us across town to one of their favorite restaurants. With a sinking feeling, we watched them wolf down a dozen hefty dishes while the possibility of a sound check steadily slipped away. Perilously close to show time, the bus crawled back to the university through gridlocked traffic. To our horror, 4,000 people were already waiting for us to take the stage.

We raced to get everything ready on stage while the impatient crowd yelled for us to begin. An hour later the concert finally commenced with a paralyzing blast of noise, causing many in the au-

*Identity Crisis in Chengdu, 1991: (L-R) Dennis Rea, Andreas Vath, Bryce Whitwam, Tom Vest (Xiao Quan)*

dience to involuntarily cover their ears in panic. Tom's frightfully overamplified drums exploded from the strained loudspeakers and ricocheted off distant buildings like cannon shots. Since this was Chengdu *Electrical* University, we had naïvely trusted the school technicians to know what they were doing, but the flustered young men acted as though they had never even flipped a light switch much less operated an arena sound system. The lack of monitor speakers made it all but impossible for us to hear each other's cues, causing us to veer badly out of sync. Every electrical device on stage was plugged into a single dangerous-looking outlet, and whenever a certain bank of stage lights came on, Bryce's keyboard mysteriously lost power. As if all this weren't bad enough, thousands of tiny flies settled on our faces, crawled up our nostrils, and swarmed over our instruments as we struggled to salvage some music from the din. (Bryce's synthesizer keys were literally black with bugs.) Partway through our nightmare set, a student singer joined us for a rendition of a Cui Jian song; the confused fellow gamely shouted the lyrics and made his best rock-star moves amid the swirling mess. Though the concert was a supreme technical embarrassment, the audience nevertheless roared in approval, showing just how starved for sensation Chinese students could be in those days.

We fared much better at a concert staged by Chengdu TV for an invited audience of local media bigwigs and government brass. The show took place at a garish new nightclub called the Shangri-La Disco, which sported a sign over its door that read "Sing and Dance Hell." Just before we took the stage, a conflict arose over the use of the name Identity Crisis. Chosen to reflect our willfully eclectic repertoire, the name had been translated by a Taiwanese friend as *zi wo fang zhu*, or "banished souls," her best stab at a synonym. Chengdu TV censors interpreted this as subversive and allowed us to play only on the condition that we appear under the name Dennis and His Friends, much to the annoyance of my bandmates.

It wasn't the first time our name had caused us trouble. Officials invariably asked us why we had chosen such a politically suspect moniker, and made us write out our song lyrics for official scrutiny. Aware that the thought police would not look kindly on tunes like "P.L.A. Boy," we instead handed over censor-friendly phonetic approximations of the real lyrics; for instance, "gone shopping" in place of "Deng Xiaoping." Once on stage, we went ahead and sang the original lyrics anyway, correctly guessing that nobody would understand a word we were saying. The show was later broadcast throughout metropolitan Chengdu, proscribed lyrics and all. Viewing the videotape months later, I cracked up at the sight of the English-speaking MC announcing the title of our song "Hot Bottom" with great seriousness.

While in Chengdu, we were also invited to perform at the 5,000-seat Worker's Cultural Palace as part of a musical equipment expo set up by Hong Kong–based retailer Tom Lee Music. The band was pumped at the prospect of playing for another large audience, but on the day of the concert we showed up at an inexplicably empty arena and met with an extremely frosty reception from the event organizers. We had arrived a day late because of a faulty translation, causing the sponsors great embarrassment. We were further mortified to discover that they had even hung a giant banner above the stage that read, "Welcome Identity Crisis!"

Pleased with the surprising success of my solo album *Shadow in Dreams*, my former record producer Yang Shichun brought Identity Crisis into the China Record Company studio to record an album for the label. The hastily arranged session yielded excellent results despite lengthy power outages on each of the three days we were in the studio. We viewed this opportunity to release a recording in China as the culmination of a tour that had already exceeded our most optimistic expectations, notwithstanding disasters like the Electrical University debacle. Alas, the album's release was ultimately blocked by China Record Company officials in Beijing, who were irked at Yang's decision to record foreign musicians without their say-so. I remain very grateful to Yang and his staff for having the audacity to attempt such a risky venture.

Before we left Chengdu, Yang urged us to meet with his music-biz colleague Feng Xiao Cong when we passed through the city of Guangzhou on our trip home. A top executive with the Guangzhou branch of the China Record Company, Feng was one of the most sought-after producers in China and pulled in an astronomical income from private productions on the side. Confident that Feng would make us an offer we couldn't refuse, Yang called ahead to arrange a rendezvous. We also hoped that Feng would be able to set up a last-minute show for us in Guangzhou. Our business in Chengdu now finished, we took leave of our friends and flew to the booming southeastern port city aboard a China Airlines jet, a luxury made possible by the modest sum we'd received for the recording session.

Feng collected us at the airport in an official China Record Company bus, complete with driver, and before we had even finished exchanging pleasantries he was already discussing a record date. He brought us to his luxurious multistory apartment, listened to a brief sample of the tape we'd just made in Chengdu, and then treated us to an expensive banquet at a classy restaurant. After the meal he showed us around the company's Guangzhou studio, the most sophisticated recording facility I'd yet seen in China. As evening approached we asked Feng to recommend an affordable place to stay for the night. He insisted on checking us into an upmarket hotel that was way out of our price range, but as we assumed he was footing the bill, we gladly availed ourselves of the swank establishment's comforts. We were genuinely mystified that this pop-music mogul was showing such an interest in our offbeat music and wondered if there was some kind of catch.

After supper Feng took us to see the house band at the cavernous Poton 100 Club, cheekily named for its outrageous cover charge of 100 RMB, about triple what most Chinese workers earned in a month. He flatly stated that the group was "the best band in China," not the first time we'd heard such a claim. Strangely, in a country where socialism had supposedly leveled the playing field, many Chinese I met seemed obsessed with rank—so-and-so is the Number 1 guitarist in town, this other guy is Number 2, and so on—although the criteria by which musicians were ranked was never very clear, and the various factions were seldom in agreement.

The traditional rivalry between Beijing and Guangzhou, or more accurately between northern and southern China, seemingly carried over into the musical sphere as well. The typical argument went that Beijing, as China's cultural capital, boasted the more original, "artistic" musicians, while Guangzhou, as the country's commercial center, produced players who were less creative but more advanced in technical ability. (Shanghai had yet to emerge as a cultural center of consequence.) While generalizations of this sort are seldom useful, the stereotype was definitely borne out by the much-hyped band we saw in Guangzhou, a collection of highly accomplished musicians wasting their talents on stylized, formulaic pop. The exhilaration we'd felt in Beijing, the sense of participating in a fugitive movement, was entirely lacking in blasé Guangzhou. To be fair, we did find the musicians helpful and personable, especially Lao Zai (a.k.a. "Loud Boy"), the finest electric guitarist I'd yet heard in China. My bandmates and I politely applauded as the group backed up a succession of extravagantly costumed male and female singers serving up the usual Hong Kong/Taiwan pop fare, not to mention a perfectly sterile rendition of Cui Jian's "Yi Wu Suo You." After their set, the band invited us on stage to play a few numbers, to their evident enjoyment.

The next morning Mr. Feng confirmed our suspicions when he dropped by our hotel and told us he regretted that we did not play more pop-friendly fare. He did encourage us to get back in touch with him after we worked up more appropriate material, but we sensed that the offer was insincere. Naturally, we got stuck with the hefty hotel bill. We then headed back to Taiwan via Hong Kong, exhausted but well satisfied with the results of our strange month-long underground concert tour.

Some weeks after our return to Taiwan, a friend in Chengdu sent me the following article from *Sichuan Youth Daily*, one of the few translated reviews of my musical activities from a Chinese point of view:

### Music Makes It All Come True

"Identity Crisis" in Chengdu, by Yang Bing

Maybe it's the lure of Sichuan itself, or perhaps it's the spirit of this city, its people, and its music which brought the band Identity Crisis to Chengdu. Founded by three American musicians and one German musician, Identity Crisis brought their fascinating, unique sound to Chengdu last month, speaking to us through the universal language of music.

For an all-too-short 10 days, thousands of people here in Chengdu flocked to their concerts and enjoyed their sounds. Chengdu Television's "Weekend Edition" also did a special feature on the band, and China Records was quick to get Identity Crisis into the studio to record an album.

Identity Crisis covered all the bases at their shows, performing many styles of Western and Eastern music, from contemporary to classical. Their philosophy is that each style has its own strength of character, and by performing diverse styles they can get closer to a core understanding of the living spirit of music. Among the selections which Identity Crisis has composed or arranged can be found jazz, rock, and Chinese traditional music. At each of their performances the band received explosive applause, particularly for new arrangements of such Chinese folk classics as "Mu Yang Qu" and "Yizu Wuqu."

This group of musicians finds Chinese music deeply fascinating and intricately beautiful. The fusion of Chinese and Western music is among their greatest interests.

Guitarist and lead singer Dennis was at Chengdu University of Science and Technology last year teaching English. During this time he was greatly influenced by Chinese music and wrote new arrangements of "Hong Bo Qu," "Yizu Wuqu," and others. At this time he also composed "Chengdu Blues," "Hot Pot," "Chopsticks Variations," and other contemporary pieces, as well as recording his first solo tape, "Shadow in Dreams." Last month, Dennis added his arrangement of the theme to *The Last Emperor* to his repertoire.

Band members Andreas, Bryce, and Tom handle the bass, keyboards, and drums respectively. They have all studied Chinese and have a great interest in Chinese culture. The group says that coming to China was a long-held wish come true. The exchange of music and ideas, making friends, playing with Chinese musicians, and working among the Chinese creative community has been an unparalleled experience for them. In the course of their independently produced tour, Identity Crisis performed with Cui Jian and Liang He Ping and played four or five concerts in Beijing. The band gave another five free concerts in Chengdu, at Chengdu University of Science and Technology, Western Medical University, and Electrical University. Their concerts were an unbroken chain of successes closing the gap between East and West and building a bridge between us and them.

Despite the flowery, self-congratulatory tone so typical of the official Chinese media, I was genuinely touched by the author's assertion that our virtually unknown band had succeeded in establishing a constructive musical dialogue across a daunting cultural divide, if only for a few brief days.

# CHAPTER 16

# THE FEELMORE EAST

Upon returning to Taiwan after the tour, we found our reputations greatly enlarged by our exploits in China and association with Cui Jian. (Everybody in Taiwan loved Cui Jian for being a thorn in the Chinese government's side, though hardly anyone actually listened to his music.) Before long the band's newfound prestige garnered us numerous invitations to play at pubs, festivals, and cultural centers in the Tainan area.

The first of these engagements was a weekly slot at the Rainy Season Pub, a cozy basement nightspot popular with the college crowd. The venue's tiny stage was far too cramped to accommodate a drum set, but we decided to take the gig anyway and have Tom play a bright-red Buddhist hand drum in lieu of a full kit. One day when bicycling around town, I noticed a sidewalk toy vendor selling a foot-high black plastic drum set emblazoned with the words "Jazz Drum." The kit comprised a diminutive bass drum about the size of a cookie tin, a six-inch snare, and a cymbal no larger than an English muffin. At a mere US$5, I couldn't resist buying it for Tom as a gag. To everyone's surprise, the toy drums didn't sound half bad, so Tom took to playing them at the Rainy Season with the aid of a microphone. He cut quite the figure sitting cross-legged on the floor, pounding away at his Lilliputian drums with yellow plastic sticks the size of pencils.

The Jazz Drums also came in handy during our occasional forays into the city's night markets. A few expatriates had discovered that they could make good money singing folk songs at these bustling nocturnal bazaars, so my bandmates and I figured we might as well get in on the action. One muggy night we rode out to a busy open-air market on the edge of town with compact amplifiers and Tom's baby drum kit strapped to our scooters and bicycles. After persuading a pineapple vendor to let us plug our equipment into his portable generator, we played a full set of Identity Crisis material for the shoppers, complete with outlandish electronic effects. Surprised at the unexpected apparition of a foreign rock band in their midst, passersby gave us more money in two hours than we usually made in a week of teaching English.

Identity Crisis proved to be such a draw at the Rainy Season Pub that the owner of the rival Pioneer Bar soon offered us a higher bid for our services. Like most other venues on the island, the Pioneer Bar relied chiefly on Filipino musicians to entertain its clientele. These experts at musical mimicry were widely considered the most talented players in East Asia and were ubiquitous at nightclubs and hotel lounges from Seoul to Singapore. Unfortunately for Taiwanese impresarios, the ROC government had recently deported most of the Filipino musicians as part of a crackdown on illegal foreign workers, leaving nightspots like the Pioneer Bar desperate for replacements. Apparently thinking that any foreign musicians would do, the proprietor of the Pioneer Bar invited us to play at her mainstream establishment three nights a week without having heard a note of our music.

Fairly certain that our eccentric instrumentals wouldn't go down well with bar patrons accustomed to hearing Filipino renditions of Lionel Ritchie and Whitney Houston, we encouraged the owner, an attractive, 30ish woman who chain-smoked like she had a death wish, to take in one of our gigs at the Rainy Season and judge for herself. Surprisingly unfazed by our intentionally strident set, she insisted that we follow her down to the Pioneer Bar, a mock cowboy saloon done up with rustic Wild West timbers, where she plied us with rounds of free Heinekens and offered us a handsome fee to accept the engagement. I had a bad feeling about the whole business and tried my damnedest to dissuade her from hiring us, but the woman was so anxious to lure customers back that she ignored all discussion of appropriate musical style. By now my bandmates had warmed to the idea of a regular high-paying gig and were urging me to compromise. Bryce proposed that we come up with a set of accessible yet intelligent pop tunes by the likes of the Police and U2, and even volunteered to sing a few numbers. Outvoted, I reluctantly agreed to accept the gig.

Over the next few days we worked up reasonably convincing renditions of songs by Peter Gabriel, Talking Heads, and other creative rock artists. Though it cut against my grain to play well-worn cover tunes, I went along with the experiment for the sake of my bandmates, who didn't share my purist pretensions. In any event, when we aired the new set on our first night at the Pioneer Bar, the borrowed material sounded contrived and insincere from the first downbeat. Bryce's flat vocal delivery didn't help, nor did the fact that I had unwisely ingested a tab of LSD before the performance. (The expatriate who'd given it to me had already gleefully informed half the audience of my condition.) In this discombobulated and painfully self-conscious state, I struggled to play the songs correctly while a hammy Bryce danced with an infant in front of the stage, microphone in hand. But our ill-advised experiment clearly wasn't working, so after four or five songs we staged a spontaneous mutiny and went back to playing our usual material, rapidly clearing the dance floor of all patrons save an elderly Taiwanese couple who happily danced ballroom-style to our grinding heavy-metal dirge "Obsidian." After a couple more weeks of playing to near-empty houses, the owner fired us for precisely the same reasons that I had warned her not to hire us in the first place.

Despite the increased playing opportunities, we were still basically an isolated phenomenon in provincial Tainan. Flush with our recent success in China, we decided the time was ripe to bring our act to big-city Taipei, where we hoped to find a hipper audience and perhaps even score a record deal.

Our old pal Dirty Roger recommended us to his friend A-Da Im, the owner of Crystal Records, Taiwan's most adventurous record company and an oasis of unconventional music in a country dominated by cloying musical confectionary. At the time, Crystal provided a vital alternative to the musical status quo by importing and distributing select foreign releases and by promoting imaginative Taiwanese artists who would otherwise have had few, if any, opportunities to record their music. The label enjoyed modest commercial success, thanks largely to its two most important acts, Taiwanese folk legend Chen Ming-chang and bad-boy rocker "Sissy" from the proto-punk band Double X. By all appearances, Crystal was a model independent enterprise that promised to be an excellent fit for our unusual music. Roger put us in touch with A-Da, who showed immediate interest in the band and scheduled a meeting to discuss a possible record deal.

A week later we turned up at Crystal's Taipei office armed with our China Record Company tape and a video clip of Identity Crisis on stage with Cui Jian in Beijing. Within minutes an impressed A-Da scheduled a recording session for later that summer. We were jubilant, amazed at how quickly things were moving along.

After we'd taken care of business, A-Da proudly put on a new Crystal release by a Taipei-based expat band with the oxymoronic name Jazz Cowboys. I was highly skeptical at first, as all of the foreign groups I'd previously heard in Taipei were dreadful top-40 cover bands like the Diplomats and M.I.T. ("Made in Taiwan"). In our isolation, we had imagined that our band was totally unique in Taiwan, but hearing the Jazz Cowboys CD quickly cured us of our hubris. Here was a crack instrumental outfit playing an imaginative blend of jazz, rock, and funk with the occasional Chinese twist, and what's more, they wrote all their own material.

Having succeeded in scoring a record deal, we turned to scouting for gig opportunities in Taipei. A-Da had suggested trying our luck at the new Feelmore Jazz Pub in the city's university district, where the Jazz Cowboys and other foreign and local jazz bands played regularly. We went directly to the Feelmore and pitched our band to the owner, hoping to impress him with our China tour and our brand-new Crystal Records deal. He promptly offered us a plum engagement playing every Saturday night for the next two months.

The Jazz Cowboys played the Feelmore that night and were every bit as good live as on their CD. Particularly striking was the playing of George Soler on the Chapman Stick, a 10-string fretted instrument that covers the range of both guitar and bass and is played by tapping on the strings with both hands, almost like playing a piano. I was so taken with George's imaginative and soulful playing that I introduced myself between sets and straightaway asked if he'd like to tour China. It was the beginning of a lasting friendship and musical partnership that eventually did culminate in a shared concert tour of China several years later.

Throughout the summer Identity Crisis enjoyed a successful and stimulating weekly residency at the Feelmore, proffering original tunes like "Manifest Density" alongside offbeat covers by the likes of Thelonius Monk. By this time Tom Vest had returned to Virginia, soon to become a father; his able replacement was the young "Spike" Tsao Hsin, an erstwhile heavy-metal warrior who proved a surprisingly deft jazz sticksman. Unlike our typical gigs in strait-laced Tainan, the Feelmore shows were packed with enthusiastic Chinese jazz fans that appreciated our peculiar music and yelled for more. Adding to the fun were occasional cameo appearances by accomplished players like Jazz Cowboys trumpeter Dominic Rablah and saxophonist Paul Chenard. For a brief season the Feelmore was the hub of a minor musical renaissance in Taipei, with half a dozen respectable jazz groups playing most nights of the week. The downside of the engagement was the weekly 400-mile round-trip journey between Tainan and Taipei on the notorious wild-chicken bus, tortured by nonstop video reruns of the comedian Chu-ke Liang, a sort of Taiwanese Benny Hill who sported a bowl haircut reminiscent of Moe from the Three Stooges.

In August 1991, Identity Crisis began recording a CD for Crystal Records at Life Studios in Taipei, with Jazz Cowboys' George Soler in the producer's chair. A daylong session yielded enough tracks for a respectable CD, but the finishing touches would have to wait until later, as I now had to attend to another unlikely concert tour of China.

*Design by Francesca Sundsten*

# CHAPTER 17

# THE VAGARIES OF TOURING CHINA

In the fall of 1991, I finally realized my long-held aim of bringing a group of top-notch American musicians to China for a concert tour. The breakthrough came when I received an invitation to perform in the China International TV Festival, a major media showcase hosted alternately by the cities of Shanghai and Chengdu. This was no run-of-the-mill gig—the opening ceremony was to be broadcast to hundreds of millions of viewers throughout China.

The invitation was finessed by Tang Lei's friend Dong Hong, a Chengdu English teacher who'd signed on with the festival as an interpreter. On hearing that the organizing committee was seeking international acts, Dong proposed that sponsors Sichuan TV invite me to represent the United States. Since the station was aware of my earlier activities in Chengdu, they reasoned that as a "friend of China" I already had the stamp of approval from local government and would be easy to work with. But the invitation still needed to be cleared by officials from China Central TV (CCTV) in Beijing, so Dong Hong arranged for me to meet with a screening committee when Identity Crisis passed through Chengdu in April of that year.

With Dong acting as translator, the committee grilled me about my music and made sure to emphasize that the government didn't want any rock music on the program. The discussion might have ended right there had I not hastened to assure them that the Vagaries, as I had named my putative band, were not a rock group. This wasn't entirely true, for however wide-ranging the band's material might be, we'd be playing electric instruments at high volume and would surely look like a rock band to government censors. Hoping to avoid an impasse, I spontaneously suggested that the Vagaries perform a piece of Chinese traditional music adapted for electric instruments. The visibly relieved officials heartily endorsed this proposal, and I sensed that I'd cleared the biggest hurdle. Before leaving, I gave the committee my contact information and promised to get back to them soon to iron out the details.

I had passed the first test, but several formidable obstacles remained. For one thing, I had conveniently neglected to tell the committee that the band I was offering didn't even exist yet. My plan all along had been to form a new group specifically for the occasion, made up of the best musicians I could recruit, but I couldn't tell the committee this without jeopardizing our participation. Somehow I had to satisfy their request for audio and video demo tapes of my nonexistent band. They also wanted to know what "work unit" we belonged to and requested proof of our affiliation with a legitimate organization. On top of all this, for political reasons I had to conceal the fact that I currently lived in Taiwan.

I eventually solved all of these problems thanks to good old American sleight of hand. Coming up with an audio demo tape was the easiest part—I simply compiled a cassette of songs from the individual band members' various projects and passed them off as the Vagaries. Providing a videotape of a fictional band was far more problematic, but I managed this by submitting long-range footage of an Identity Crisis concert, gambling that the committee wouldn't notice that it was a different band—or that it had been taped in Chengdu! (They didn't.) As for our "work unit," band member Roland Barker's partner, Lisa Dutton, let us use her Seattle-based film-production enterprise, Motherland Productions (now rechristened a "performing arts management company"), as an umbrella for the band's activities. Finally, I concealed the fact that I lived in Taiwan by triangulating all festival correspondence from Tainan to Seattle to Chengdu and back again by using Motherland's fax machine and letterhead. Lisa proved indispensable to the tour's success, taking on a large part of the planning and fundraising and acting as the band's co-manager in China.

The Vagaries were keyboardist/saxophonist Roland Barker, drummer Bill Rieflin, keyboardist/vocalist Charley Rowan, and electric bassist Mike Davidson. I had worked previously with Roland and Bill on Roland's soundtrack to the 1988 cult film *Shredder Orpheus* and felt it was a musical relationship worth continuing. Charley and

*The Vagaries: (L-R): Charley Rowan, William Rieflin, Dennis Rea, Mike Davidson, Roland Barker (Spike Mafford)*

I had a long history of working together in various groups in Seattle. Mike had played with both Bill and Roland in influential early '80s Seattle band the Blackouts, which later evolved into industrial rock giants Ministry. All four players were highly regarded instrumentalists and songwriters, with distinct but complementary sensibilities. I was sure they would be unique in China and felt greatly honored that they had accepted my invitation on faith. My idea was for each band member to contribute original material with our particular instrumentation and strengths in mind. Based on past experience playing in China, I recommended that the band develop a wide-ranging repertoire in order to expose our audiences to the greatest variety of musical styles.

In due course the festival sent us our official invitation. Now we could turn our attention to the next challenge, namely, raising enough money to make the trip over from the States. The festival had agreed to cover our in-China expenses, including round-trip airfare between our point of entry (Guangzhou) and Chengdu, but getting to China was our own responsibility, and none of us had the resources to cover trans-Pacific flights. Fortunately, a musician friend in Seattle steered me to Arts International, a funding organization that awarded travel grants to U.S. artists performing in arts festivals abroad. Since few American creative musicians had ever played for a national television audience in Mainland China, Arts International readily underwrote the Vagaries' round-trip airfare to Hong Kong. I savored the irony of being paid to play subversive music by both the U.S. and Chinese governments. Additional support came from the Washington State China Relations Council and, oddly, the Seattle-based Muzak Corporation. We earned extra pocket money through a fundraiser concert we played in Seattle and from sales of handsome Vagaries China Tour T-shirts designed by Bill's partner, the gifted artist Francesca (Frankie) Sundsten. Our money problems now solved, I set to work arranging additional shows for the band in other Chinese cities with the assistance of Tang Lei, now living in Germany.

In late August, just after wrapping up the Identity Crisis recording session for Crystal Records in Taipei, I flew to Seattle for three weeks of intensive rehearsals with the Vagaries. Now came the real test: Could an artificially contrived band that had never played together as a unit create music compelling enough to justify our appearance in a high-profile international festival? To my great relief, the band quickly hit its stride and managed to put together a solid set of original material that ranged from twisted jazz to edgy art-rock to moody electronic music, with a couple of vocal numbers to round things out.

The novelty of a local rock band touring China generated a fair amount of interest in the Seattle music community and garnered us a number of write-ups in the press. Convinced that our cross-cultural adventure would make a perfect subject for a documentary, Lisa proposed bringing along a small film crew to capture our concerts and the Chinese music scene in general. I thought this was a terrific idea but feared that suspicious authorities would confiscate our film equipment. To guard against this possibility, Lisa and her assistant, Daniel, acquired the smallest video camera possible and slyly entered it on the equipment list we submitted to Chinese Customs, explaining that it would only be used to record the Vagaries' festival performance. After months of delicate negotiation and preparation, we were finally ready to take flight across the Pacific.

In late September the Vagaries alighted in Hong Kong with an entourage that included Lisa, Daniel, Frankie, photographer Spike Mafford, and friends Heather Kennedy and Deborah Pops—11 people in all. Too small-time to enjoy the luxury of a road crew, we got an immediate taste of what was to come as we dragged around our heaps of unwieldy baggage, including a snare drum, cymbals, two keyboards, two guitars, racks of musical accessories, camera equipment, and a couple dozen suitcases and backpacks. After two nights at the surreal Chungking Mansions, a block-square firetrap crammed with budget hotels and itinerant peddlers from all over the globe, we took a train across the border to Guangzhou to begin the tour in earnest. We were met at the station by a festival representative and an employee of Guangdong provincial TV, who treated us to the first of many sumptuous meals we would enjoy during the band's stay in China and gave us a perfunctory city tour before seeing us onto a late-afternoon flight to Chengdu.

A few hours later we touched down at the Chengdu airport to

find a welcoming committee of TV cameramen, newspaper reporters, and festival staff awaiting us on the chilly tarmac. We could hardly believe that people were lavishing this much attention on a band that existed only in a phony press kit, but such was the stir created by foreign artists in those days.

The uncharacteristically tidy city was aswirl with all manner of festival hoopla. Street lamps were festooned with banners and lanterns, tourists and dignitaries abounded, and villagers from the surrounding countryside thronged the streets hawking local handicrafts. It looked like half of Sichuan Province had converged on Chengdu to join in the revelry or make a buck off the festival.

When our chaperones checked us into our rooms at the upscale Minshan Hotel, a festival functionary greeted us with the news that some of our instruments had not been registered properly with customs and were therefore contraband. The matter was eventually ironed out, but not before several anxious days of sweating over whether our keyboards would be seized.

In the morning a festival official named Guo Yang showed up at the hotel and instructed us to report to the imposing Sichuan Provincial Arena for a dress rehearsal. Grateful for the chance to get in some badly needed band practice before the festival commenced, we loaded our instruments into a shuttle bus and drove to the massive venue, where we found Guo Yang and a cadre of festival dignitaries awaiting us. When we asked about setting up our gear, Guo Yang delivered the stunning news that the band would not perform live, as previously agreed, but would have to fake playing along to a prerecorded tape! Although we had furnished a detailed list of our equipment needs months earlier at the festival's request, it was now clear that the organizers had never intended to let a foreign band play live on national television. We objected vigorously, only to be curtly silenced by a surly P.L.A. officer in full uniform. Guo Yang then disclosed that the evening's "dress rehearsal" was in fact a public concert—for 10,000 people.

Far from playing a live set of creative instrumental music on nationwide TV, we would now have to suffer the embarrassment of miming to canned music. And since the band had only materialized a few weeks earlier, we didn't even have any tapes to offer the organizers. Miffed that we hadn't brought any recordings, Guo Yang, whose face seemed frozen in a perpetual scowl, commanded us to record two songs that very afternoon at Sichuan Radio. He handed us over to a functionary from China Central TV, who instructed us to record "one Chinese song and one country-western song" and then hastened to add, "and no rock music!" Country-western? His request left us speechless; we had never played a lick of country music in our lives and had little desire to reinvent ourselves now.

The CCTV escort hustled us onto a minibus for the drive across town to Sichuan Radio's studio, a dark, frigid mausoleum of a room where I'd recorded tracks for the radio station back in 1989. At a loss to satisfy the festival's ill-timed request for a country tune, we decided on Charley's "I Was Wrong," a melodic vocal number that we hoped would pass for C&W at this geographical distance. But even this inoffensive tune was uncomfortably close to rock, with its climax built on booming drums and revved-up electric guitar. We auditioned the song for our hosts in the studio, bracing ourselves for the inevitable thumbs-down. As the final power chord ebbed into silence, the CCTV watchdog suddenly exclaimed, "Yes! That's exactly what we're looking for!" Fortunately for us, this Party apparatchik didn't know country music from break dancing.

Handicapped by one-eared headphones and crackling wires, we recorded a stiff version of "I Was Wrong" plus my elaborate arrangement of the traditional folk piece "Dance Song of the Yi People." The session wrapped up just three hours before show time. Since we weren't allowed to participate in mixing the songs, we wouldn't even get to hear the finished product until we were actually on stage.

The so-called dress rehearsal was in actuality a public preview of the festival's opening ceremony, a rococo extravaganza boasting a cast of hundreds. Based on the theme "the Western Nationalities," the ceremony was a veritable sideshow featuring a dozen ethnic minority groups native to western China—Uighurs, Tibetans, Miaos, and others—all decked out in traditional finery. Most of these performers belonged to state-sponsored song-and-dance ensembles that regularly toured provincial capitals to promote the government's fatuous claims of ethnic unity. The festival lineup was rounded out by a troupe of People's Liberation Army acrobats, the State Dance Company of Belarus, a popular Taiwanese pop singer, a traditional *xiangsheng* comedy duo, and scores of adorable preteen girls costumed as red Sichuan chili peppers, complete with green-stemmed headgear. The backstage scene was reminiscent of a Fellini film, with dozens of musicians and dancers mingling in riotously colored garments. Meeting these friendly, unassuming people was definitely the highlight of our festival experience. One especially touching moment

*Sichuan-China International TV Festival curtain call (Spike Mafford)*

came when an admiring Uighur drummer presented Bill with the gift of a grim-looking dagger, a token of high regard in his culture.

The spectacle kicked off with superstar pop songstress and P.L.A. soldier Mao Aming singing the festival's theme song, "Love Spreads All Over the World," a maudlin ditty that climaxed on the word "television" sung in English. After a few more acts we walked on stage to the cheering of thousands, feeling utterly fraudulent with our unplugged instruments in hand. The recording engineers had inserted a four-beat cue before the first song so we would know when to begin, but the soundman carelessly rolled the tape on the second beat, forcing us to lurch awkwardly to a late start. Now everyone could see that we weren't really playing. Worse still, the Sichuan Radio mixing engineers had mutilated our songs almost beyond recognition. Thoroughly dispirited, we struck our mute instruments mechanically and emoted insincerely against a backdrop of giant mushroom-shaped fiberglass stage props right out of *This Is Spinal Tap*. A few minutes later the humiliating exercise was over. We slunk offstage feeling like complete charlatans.

The next morning an irritable Guo Yang summoned us to a meeting and announced that a second "dress rehearsal" would take place that evening, that we should be more "active" on stage, and that our time slot was being cut back from 10 to 3½ minutes because the festival program supposedly was too long. Ironically, he told us to drop my arrangement of "Dance Song of the Yi People," the traditional piece that had gotten us the gig in the first place; it was now considered too cerebral and "not Western enough." After having been expressly forbidden from playing rock music, our sole contribution to the festival would now be a rock song.

The once-cordial festival organizers had grown ominously cool toward us. When we asked Dong Hong if we'd inadvertently done anything to anger them, she confided that some Communist Party officials were outraged at the discovery that we were indeed a dreaded rock band and not a group of smiley-faced Foreign Friends playing harmless Chinese folk tunes. I'm sure that they'd have pulled us from the program altogether if it wouldn't have meant a major loss of face for the organizers who'd invited us.

We did manage to persuade Guo Yang to let us return to the studio to remix the tape, this time with better results. During the mixing session my former manager Tang Lei unexpectedly materialized from Germany, where she'd been studying in a language program. She could hardly have chosen a more opportune moment to appear, given the many communication breakdowns we were experiencing. She quickly took control of the situation and also set to work arranging our post-festival tour itinerary.

The band repeated the pantomime at the second sold-out preview show and again the following day in the official festival opening ceremony, watched by a TV audience estimated in the hundreds of millions, including viewers in Mongolia, Pakistan, and other countries bordering China. Normally we would have been thrilled at this incredible exposure, but our satisfaction was tempered by the knowledge that we'd been reduced to lip-synching like some pop combo on *American Bandstand*.

We had failed to achieve our audacious goal of broadcasting challenging live instrumental music into the homes of viewers throughout China, but we weren't finished yet. The opening ceremony was followed by two "congratulatory performances" at the sold-out arena; now that we no longer posed a moral threat to a national television audience, officials finally agreed to let us perform six songs in real time. On the afternoon of the first show, we arrived at the arena for a sound check only to find the promised instrument amplifiers missing. The soundman tried to persuade us to plug directly into the arena-size PA system, but we politely refused, not wanting to risk another disaster like the Identity Crisis concert at Chengdu Electrical University earlier that year. A festival representative reluctantly drove us to a music shop to borrow some amplifiers, but since the only amps available were of a different brand than the PA equipment used by the festival, the rep decreed that we couldn't use them without infringing on the PA manufacturer's advertising monopoly. We ended up using a separate PA system for each band member—enough wattage to power five bands.

The band nevertheless turned in its first truly representative performance in China, and we exacted a small measure of revenge on Guo Yang by playing longer than we had agreed, rushing into an extra number as the soundman frantically gestured for us to stop; after all, we'd been hoodwinked into delivering five gigantic concerts for the price of one. Since arriving in Chengdu a week earlier, the Vagaries had not only appeared in front of a nationwide TV audience, per our original agreement, but had also performed for nearly 50,000 concertgoers and, in the televised final congratulatory concert, millions of additional viewers throughout Sichuan Province.

After the last arena concert we ditched our festival chaperones and hauled our gear down to the Jinhe Hotel, where my old guitarist pal Zhou Di and his band Hei Ma were throwing a semiprivate rock and roll party in the hotel disco. Fed up with festival politics, we took full advantage of this opportunity to blow out our frustrations and played a loud, unrestricted set. The young musicians and their friends crowded onto the stage with us, whooping with glee and drowning us in tepid Lüye beer.

Informal gigs like the Jinhe party, which involved actual human contact, interested us far more than the sterile pomp of stagy propaganda events like the Sichuan-China International TV Festival. Thinking it would be a terrible waste to travel all the way to China just to make a 4-minute cameo appearance on a strictly controlled government TV special, we had lobbied festival organizers for months to book us additional public concerts. On arriving in Chengdu, we were thrilled to learn that the organizers had scheduled two shows for us at the enormous Workers' Cultural Palace. We were really looking forward to playing unadulterated sets at these shows, but as soon as we fulfilled our obligation to the festival, Guo

Yang announced that the concerts had been canceled because the Cultural Palace was reserved for other activities.

In compensation he offered us a small concert in the provincial backwater of Luzhou, a 10-hour bus ride from Chengdu. We exploded in protest, certain that he was yanking our chain. A discreet investigation by Tang Lei revealed that Guo Yang had tried to extort a princely sum from the Cultural Palace for letting us play there, and the venue had understandably declined. Appalled that China's premier media event would shamelessly capitalize on its international guests in this manner, we refused the show in Luzhou and let Guo Yang know exactly how we felt about his profiteering. Unfortunately, the task of translating fell to the already overstressed Dong Hong, who was mortified at being caught between her Party superiors and some testy foreign musicians. We eventually settled on playing three afternoon shows in the tiny Minshan Hotel disco for an audience made up mostly of petty gangsters. It came out that the avaricious festival organizers were charging an exorbitant 30 RMB at the door (most concerts cost less than 5 RMB) while telling us the concerts were free. And in a final display of contempt for the foreign guests, the oily Guo Yang even tried to slip away from Chengdu without paying our return airfare as promised—thankfully, we were tipped off by a sympathetic source in time.

Government officials were obviously trying their damnedest to shield the public from us, and vice versa. The Sichuan-China *International* TV Festival was not a happy experience for the Vagaries, but our stay in Chengdu ended on a positive note with an underground concert at the capacious Night Salon disco. About 500 people turned up to watch us play on an outlandish two-level wedding cake of a stage crowded with thick pillars that made it nearly impossible for us to see and hear each other. Despite this impediment, we delivered a vigorous set, and the audience reacted so wildly that the frightened club owner asked us to cut our performance short, afraid that the overexcited patrons would trash his disco.

Though we'd been taken for dupes by the politicos that ran the festival, we had the last laugh in the end. Believing that the ignorant American musicians had gone back home, Guo Yang and his cronies never found out that we used their invitation as a springboard for a month-long guerilla tour of four Chinese cities, sowing viral seeds of unauthorized music wherever we played.

*The Vagaries play the 'wedding cake' stage, Night Salon Disco, Chengdu 1991 (Spike Mafford)*

# CHAPTER 18

# "THE POWER OF ROCK AND ROLL"

The Vagaries traveled on to Chongqing aboard a pocket-size China Airlines jet, buffeted by frightful air turbulence throughout the short journey to the fogbound Yangtze River port city. Our entourage had now grown to include Anne, who'd flown in from Taiwan for the occasion; Tang Lei, now acting as our road manager; and my friend Jiang Zhicheng, an employee of the China Travel Service, with his new bride—15 people in all, a ridiculously cumbersome party for what had been conceived as a stealth concert tour of a still politically sensitive China.

We were extremely grateful to be out from under the watchful gaze of TV festival officials, but challenges still awaited us at every turn. Despite her best efforts, Tang Lei was thwarted in her attempt to arrange a Vagaries concert at Southwest China Art Academy in Chongqing, despite my having played a well-received solo concert there the previous year, for the political climate at universities had grown perceptibly frostier since the Identity Crisis tour just six months earlier. Even though we had already appeared on TV sets all across China, booking more gigs was proving to be a major trial. One factor was doubtless the recent collapse of world communism, which had sent tremors of paranoia through China's leadership, especially since the summary execution of Romanian dictator Nicolae Ceaucescu. Authorities citing "new regulations" shot down three prospective dates in the relatively freewheeling city of Shenzhen, adjacent to Hong Kong. A potential gig in Shanghai fell through for similar reasons, and the word from Beijing was that the rock and roll "parties" had been all but harassed out of existence. It looked like we were going to have a hell of a time patching together a tour.

Filming our activities, on the other hand, turned out to be surprisingly hassle-free. Daniel was able to videotape virtually anything he wanted without interference from police or government officials—even meetings between Party functionaries. He would return home with more than 20 hours' worth of Vagaries performance footage, plus interviews with audience members and notable Chinese musicians. Photographer Spike Mafford likewise collected a large amount of valuable documentary material, including many of the illustrations that grace this book.

The resourceful Tang Lei salvaged the Chongqing leg of the tour by arranging shows on three consecutive nights at the Chicago Night Club, a disreputable disco that boasted a lurid Day-Glo mural of the Windy City skyline. Most of the patrons at these sparsely attended gigs were small-time wheeler-dealers who chain-smoked, downed copious amounts of cognac, and chatted loudly throughout our sets. Our biggest supporters were the house musicians, who hovered behind us on stage, craning their necks to get a better look at our fingerwork. In a rerun of so many of my earlier travails, night police officers showed up on the second and chastised the Chinese-American owner for booking a foreign band without first clearing it with the Cultural Ministry. The matter was settled the old-fashioned way—with a cash payoff—and we were allowed to finish the engagement without further harassment. My most vivid memory of these shows is the opening act, a pre-teen contortionist who tied herself into knots on a Formica tabletop while balancing a stack of plates on a spoon clenched between her teeth.

Tang Lei also persuaded the manager of the elegant Renmin Hotel, a local landmark modeled after the venerable Temple of Heaven in Beijing, to house and feed our entire party in exchange for two concerts in the hotel ballroom for roughly 500 well-heeled audience members. Before the first of these shows we discovered that our hosts had once again failed to provide the requisite instrument amplifiers, necessitating a breathless dash to a music equipment dealer in the city center. The concert was delayed another two hours as disorganized technicians fussed with a hazardous-looking bundle of wires backstage. To their credit, the audience exhibited remarkable patience during the lengthy delay. We finally got underway and were just beginning to build momentum when the power suddenly failed, leaving Bill playing an unplanned drum solo in the dark. The capper on this ill-starred gig came when I accidentally broke my guitar's bridge mechanism during the set, requiring makeshift repairs that caused serious tuning problems for the remainder of the tour.

Between gigs, we explored Chongqing's steep lanes and stairways on foot in the ever-present dirty gray mist that gives the town its descriptive appellation of Wudu, or "Fog City." Occupying a narrow promontory at the confluence of the Jinsha (upper Yangtze) and Jialing rivers, Chongqing stands apart from China's invariably flat cities on account of its mountainous topography and resultant absence of bicycles. Stone and brick buildings clung like barnacles to cliffs overlooking the swirling river waters that lap the ancient Chaotianmen wharves at the peninsula's sandy apex, giving the city an austere, medieval aspect. Just 10 years later Chongqing would look like a Chinese Manhattan, bristling with slender skyscrapers.

The next tour stop was sunny Kunming, the "City of Eternal Spring" in southwest China's Yunnan Province. Tang Lei had worked out another play-for-stay agreement with the Golden Peacock Hotel, as well as a semiprivate concert at the Yunnan Song and Dance Troupe's compound. We were greeted at the airport by a delegation from the Kunming Symphony Orchestra—talk about crossover appeal—whose conductor held up a small banner reading, "Welcome Fantasia from USA." *Fantasia?* Like Identity Crisis, the Vagaries' name caused no end of confusion. Inexplicably translated as "Strange Ideas" in Chinese, it proved a political liability throughout our tour.

The hotel manager graciously let our whole party stay at the Golden Peacock for a week in return for our doing a small invitation-only show in the hotel dancehall. Mike Davidson's girlfriend Debbie repaid the manager's kindness by forgetting to turn off the tap in their bathtub before going out one day, flooding the entire room with several inches of steaming water.

The concert we played for the Yunnan Song and Dance Troupe was among my most satisfying in China, thanks to a sympathetic audience made up mostly of professional musicians, dancers, and other artists. As capital of a distant province inhabited largely by minority nationalities, Kunming possessed a relaxed frontier atmosphere that offered a welcome contrast to the other cities we had visited; its citizens were refreshingly genial and open-minded. After the show the Kunming musicians crowded around to ply us with questions about musical equipment and playing technique, while olive-uniformed soldiers looked on in puzzlement. But the local soldiers and police weren't always so affable: On one of our sightseeing excursions in the city, we chanced to witness cops

*Audience members dancing at Vagaries concert, Kunming National Defense Arena, 1991 (Spike Mafford)*

jabbing a suspected shoplifter with a pencil compass and then pistol-whipping the poor wretch viciously with a sturdy metal coat hanger.

One afternoon we happened on the hotel manager in a huddle with some businessmen in the lobby. The excited hotelier explained that they were working to arrange a large public concert for the Vagaries at the poetically named Kunming National Defense Arena. We were highly dubious given our past record of disappointments, but the manager assured us that city officials had already granted their approval, pending final authorization by the provincial Cultural Ministry. That night members of the band dined with a delegation of Cultural Ministry officers that included a severe-looking director of propaganda resembling Madam Mao. After dinner we showed them a Vagaries performance video that Lisa and Daniel had quickly cobbled together just hours earlier. The soundtrack was so woefully distorted that we were certain the officials would reject us, but our appearance in the Sichuan-China International TV Festival apparently impressed them enough to clinch the deal.

Our October 13 concert at the National Defense Arena—also host to basketball games and public executions of condemned criminals—was unquestionably the high-water mark of the Vagaries tour, and reportedly the first-ever public rock concert in Yunnan Province. The 4,000 attendees were unrestrained in their enthusiasm, the sound was actually tolerable, and the band played a bang-up show, our best in China. Accustomed to concertgoers who typically sat motionless in their seats like wax effigies, I was exhilarated to see about a dozen young people suddenly run out onto the arena floor and begin dancing to one of our more rousing numbers. A few of the revelers got so carried away that they leapt up onto the stage and gyrated amidst the band, tripping over our effects pedals and entangling themselves in our cables. One hyperanimated fellow strutted about waving a homemade sign emblazoned with the word **ROCK** in both Chinese and English. Two youths wearing Cui Jian T-shirts did stylized dance steps at the edge of the stage, while another ecstatic fan cartwheeled across the arena floor. I was elated that we had stimulated such unruly antics, but within moments, government overseers ordered us to tell the audience to return to their seats at once or the concert would be cut short, prompting jeers from the onlookers. The dancers sullenly complied for a time. They spilled back onto the floor for our final number, but this time the officials held their peace.

After the concert our hosts escorted us to a famous local restaurant for an expansive spread of toothsome local specialties, including the curiously named Over-the-Bridge Noodles. During the celebration the provincial cultural minister, under the influence of vast quantities of beer and Chinese liquor, called a toast and memorably declared, "I have seen the power of rock and roll!"

As we were slogging around the Chinese hinterlands on our guerrilla concert tour, news arrived that Paul Simon was about to waltz over the border from Hong Kong to play a big concert in Guangzhou, making him one of only a handful of major American artists to perform in China since the communist revolution. The event was so singular that musicians from all over China were converging on Guangzhou, including many of the people we'd hoped to see in Beijing. Since a concert in the capital city might have taken as much as a month to arrange given the current political climate, and as our funds were rapidly diminishing, we opted to join the pilgrimage to Guangzhou instead.

On the two-day train trip eastward across the crumpled landscapes of southern China, we met a young rock band from Guiyang, the capital of impoverished Guizhou Province. Chasing the rock and roll chimera, the band had pulled up stakes and was moving to sophisticated Guangzhou to take a crack at the big time. The Guiyang musicians recognized us right away from our TV festival appearance and badgered us mercilessly for guitar lessons all the way to Guangzhou. Later in the journey, some students in a passing train pointed at us excitedly and played air guitar. Small world indeed.

We arrived in Guangzhou to find a virtual family reunion in progress, with Cui Jian, Liang Heping, Loud Boy, and dozens of other rock musicians from throughout the country in town to take in the Paul Simon concert. But the Vagaries didn't enjoy the clout of a Paul Simon, and setting up concerts again proved problematic. According to Loud Boy and others, even relatively liberal Guangzhou had felt a chill political wind in recent months, so we would be limited to playing private shows only. Loud Boy kindly set up two word-of-mouth gigs for us at Poton 100, site of Identity Crisis' appearance earlier that year and the default hangout for the visiting musicians.

U.S. consular officials had arranged for Cui Jian to dine with Paul Simon, who invited the Chinese rocker to make a cameo appearance with him. The two musicians agreed to duet on "Yi Wu Suo You" and Simon's "Scarborough Fair," a favorite of Cui Jian's as a teenage folksinger. The consulate also scheduled a special evening at Poton 100 to fête Simon and his band, an all-star assemblage that numbered big-name players like saxophonist Michael Brecker and drummer Steve Gadd among its members. That night the club filled up with dozens of Chinese musicians, many of whom had traveled great distances at considerable expense in the hope of meeting their heroes, but neither Simon nor his band deigned to show up. The Chinese players were visibly crestfallen, and I felt that Simon had squandered a unique opportunity to forge ties with a rising generation of creative musicians in a nation hungry for contemporary role models. He spent little more than 24 hours in the country but reaped reams of international publicity for his "groundbreaking" foray into China.

I attended the Simon concert, eager to observe the audience's reaction and Cui Jian's duet. The 8,000-seat arena was little more than half-full, doubtless owing to the 50–100 RMB ticket price, a month's wages for most Chinese at the time. Since Simon's reputation in China rested solely on early Simon and Garfunkel classics like "Bridge over Troubled Water," his hybrid Afro-Caribbean fusion was quite a leap for the visibly baffled audience. At first the crowd was typically sedate, despite the fact that someone had distributed hundreds of annoying plastic whistles. Partway into the concert the several hundred foreign students and businessmen in the audience got up and started dancing in the aisles; the Chinese in turn loosened up a bit and clapped along awkwardly to the strange music. Still, it was nothing like the spontaneous emotional release I'd witnessed at underground Vagaries and Identity Crisis shows in Kunming, Chengdu, and Beijing.

I waited impatiently for Cui Jian to join Simon on stage and at length spotted him entering the backstage area, only to emerge moments later and return to his seat for the rest of the concert. He later explained that local government officials had threatened to shut down the show altogether if he participated. He was bitterly disappointed but hardly surprised at being denied a chance to share the stage with his onetime inspiration. (Years later, Cui Jian would more than make up for this disappointment when he made a triumphant cameo appearance with the Rolling Stones in Shanghai.)

Later that night the Vagaries played a show at Poton 100 that was indisputably the weakest of our tour. We put it down to 10 days without practice, but it didn't help that my guitar was still slipping out of tune in the aftermath of the Chongqing incident, or that poor Bill had to play drums while enclosed in a bizarre Plexiglas cage. At least Simon's superstar instrumentalists weren't there to see us embarrass ourselves.

Following the debacle the club owner treated about 50 people, including Cui Jian, the Vagaries, and an assortment of Beijing and Guangzhou musicians, to dinner at a famous restaurant specializing in snake, lizard, and other fork-tongued delicacies. Amidst the merriment our photographer, Spike, already inebriated after several rounds of toasts, stunned the crowd into silence by draining a tall glass of swampwater-green snake bile liquor, poured directly from a jar containing the coiled body of the dead serpent. By the end of the festivities he was so swacked that he had to be carried back to our hostel, where he slithered up to his dormitory room and fell into a comatose sleep. He awoke the next morning to find a Pakistani woman sitting bolt upright in the opposite bed, staring at him in terror. In his stupor, Spike had mistakenly barged into the wrong dormitory of a gender-segregated hostel.

While in Guangzhou we checked in with some contacts to whom we'd been referred by the U.S. consulate in Chengdu. Intrigued by our tales of bringing progressive art-rock to the Chinese masses, the wife of the Consul General in Guangzhou invited us to their home for a much-appreciated home-cooked spaghetti dinner. After the meal we showed her some video clips of our tour, plus a short documentary about Yunnan ethnic minority rites that an independent Chinese filmmaker had given us in Kunming. A few minutes into the documentary, Roland exclaimed in disbelief that the soundtrack consisted of material he'd written years earlier in Seattle; how the director had come by Roland's unpublished material was a complete mystery. The music was eventually traced to a tape I'd given Tang Lei in Chengdu in 1989, which had been passed on to a filmmaker friend of her husband's in Chongqing and thence to Kunming, where it ended up on the documentary soundtrack. The filmmaker couldn't possibly have known when he gave us the videotape that he was handing the music back to its composer from halfway across the world. The incident ranked as one of the strangest coincidences to befall us in all the vastness of China.

On our last day in Guangzhou we played another private show at Poton 100 for local musicians. The following morning we moved on to Zhuhai, a government-designated "Special Economic Zone" adjacent to Macau, to attend a theater concert by Cui Jian's band. By this time our entourage had amassed so much additional baggage that we had to hire a 24-seat bus to contain it all. Every seat was piled nearly to the ceiling with music gear, luggage, and souvenirs, including a 24-inch gong.

Cui Jian had been mostly idle since the government pulled the plug on him midway through his controversial 1990 concert tour. The 1991 release of his second album, *Solution*, did little to improve relations with the authorities, containing as it did both the sacrilegious "Nanniwan" and the provocative "Last Shot." He lamented that all his band did was rehearse and was afraid his musicians would lose heart. We were therefore delighted to learn that he had managed to book two sizable concerts in this pleasant coastal resort, just a short bus ride from Guangzhou and conveniently located on our route out of the country.

The Vagaries showed up in Zhuhai to a warm welcome from Cui Jian and his band, who arranged excellent accommodations for our party at bargain rates. Better still, after conferring with his manager, Liang Weiping, Cui Jian invited us to open that night's show. We were elated at the prospect; what better way to end our tour than by playing a large concert with the legendary paragon of Chinese rock? Just to be safe, Liang Weiping dispatched a messenger to the local Cultural Ministry office to seek permission, armed with our official TV festival invitation. At length the messenger returned and reported that the office was closed for the day. Cui Jian and Liang Weiping decided to risk letting us open the show anyway, permission or no. We hurriedly collected our gear, drove to the theater, and did a sound check. About an hour before show time we walked to a nearby restaurant for a quick meal, all pumped up for our climactic appearance.

I knew something had gone awry the instant I saw a long-faced Liang Weiping walk into the restaurant and approach our table. In apologetic tones, he explained that the Cultural Ministry, having been tipped off about the unauthorized foreign band, had sent officers to the theater to prevent us from playing. If we so much as played a note, the whole concert would be canceled. At that moment I felt utterly squashed by the full weight of all our accumulated frustrations with Chinese officialdom. My bandmates likewise were thoroughly deflated. And Cui Jian, who'd been through the same song and dance countless times, understood our disappointment better than anyone else in China.

Our defeat didn't prevent Cui Jian and his band from giving an inspired concert. Visibly ecstatic at being back on stage, he had the audience cheering from the first downbeat. The concert progressed without incident until a few spectators rose to their feet and started dancing to an especially infectious number, at which a uniformed guard suddenly materialized and ordered the dancers back to their seats. The dancing resumed a few songs later, but this time the guard stormed back and physically shoved one of the revelers back into

*Backstage view of Cui Jian (center) in concert, Zhuhai 1991 (Spike Mafford)*

her seat. In an instant the entire audience rose to its feet in defiance. The air fairly sizzled with tension. Aware of the probable outcome of such a confrontation, I braced myself for the worst, but Cui Jian's crew, all seasoned veterans of this kind of showdown, soon had the matter well in hand. In a flash, the light man in the balcony trained a bright spotlight on the guard. One of Cui Jian's people appeared from out of nowhere, recording the confrontation at close range on videotape. Rattled by the crowd's reaction, the guard beat a hasty retreat and the audience danced and yelled until the final encore faded to silence. Chalk up one small but immensely satisfying victory for Chinese rock and roll.

After the concert, we all lingered well into the humid, starry night over fried octopus and many rounds of beers at a beachside restaurant. With heavy hearts, we bid adieu to China, Cui Jian, and our friends. Early the next morning we dragged our mountain of luggage over the border into Macau. The Vagaries dispersed for the last time, some flying home to Seattle and others traveling on to Bali for a well-deserved holiday, while this now-penniless guitarist sailed back to Taiwan aboard the funky old SS *Macmosa*.

# CHAPTER 19

# TAIWANNABES

Much had changed in Taiwan during the two months I'd spent in Seattle and China with the Vagaries. For starters, I returned to an unexpected and very strange new home. While I was away, Anne had been forced to move our household when our landlord, Mrs. Huang, suddenly sold the building we'd been living in. To her credit, Mrs. Huang felt badly enough about the eviction that she did better than find us a new apartment—she *built* us one.

The Huang family owned a commercial building in a downtown district redundantly known as "Chinatown," where their tenants included an upscale Western-style café and one of the city's ubiquitous 7-11 convenience stores. (I counted 10 within a five-block radius of our building.) The Huangs' answer to our housing dilemma was to construct us a brand-new two-bedroom apartment in an unused part of the building's second floor. Anne and I were very touched by this gesture of goodwill, but there was one major drawback: The apartment could only be accessed through a door in the back wall of the café. Imagine the puzzlement of the patrons at seeing foreigners, rare enough in Tainan, walk into the dining area and disappear through a door in the far wall. I could always hear the customers murmur in astonishment as I closed the door behind me.

And that wasn't the half of it. A few months after we moved in, the Huangs rented the vacant space between our apartment and the café to a Mrs. Guo, who opened a skin-care salon that offered waxing treatments, facials, and other cosmetic services to Taiwanese ladies. Now we not only had to run the gauntlet of gaping café patrons, but also had to make our way across a beauty parlor filled with reclining, towel-clad women having their pimples tweezed, only to exit through another unmarked door. The sudden appearance of a foreign man in this feminine domain gave rise to much gossipy speculation among the clients, and it soon became apparent that Mrs. Guo considered us an embarrassment and wanted us out in the worst way. It was also obvious that she coveted our apartment for an expansion of her business, but the Huangs, whose children were our English students, honorably defended our right to stay. Temporarily frustrated in her efforts to drive us away, the scheming Mrs. Guo bided her time.

The local music scene had changed as well. Several core members of the nomadic Tainan music community had left the island, including my former Identity Crisis bandmates Andreas Vath and Tsao Hsin. Meanwhile, a number of newcomers had arrived to staff the next shift, and Gang of Formosa alumnus Volker Wiedersheim had returned from Germany to spend more time with his fiancée.

Of the old guard, Mark DeForge continued to instigate musical activity. With three newly arrived recruits from his hometown in New York State—guitarist Bruce Culver, singer Tom Fris, and drummer Dave Treanor—Mark formed Misery, an abrasive, confrontational punk band that disconcerted local audiences whose tastes ran more to the likes of Lobo and Debbie Gibson. I later joined the band at Mark's invitation. A typical Misery performance would see Mark take the stage swathed in bandages from head to toe while Tom ran amok among the startled audience during tunes like "Party in the Ghetto" and "Perfect Goat Imitation." (Mark's penchant for staging disturbing spectacles had reached a climax at Lost Weekend's final show at a Tainan pub in early 1991, when he smashed a table with a flaming guitar.) Mark had also launched a bilingual alternative monthly paper, the *Modern Times*, which reported on such outré topics as graffiti, street theater, the films of David Lynch, and Tainan's underground music scene.

A number of Taiwanese rock groups were now active in the city, made up mostly of students from National Cheng Kung University. The reigning kings of the scene were Metal Fon, a formulaic heavy-metal outfit led by fiery guitarist A-Fan. At the other end of the musical spectrum were Sonic Fire, a keyboard-driven jazz fusion band that held forth weekly at the Pioneer Pub, site of Identity Crisis' ill-fated pop music experiment earlier in the year. Other Tainan bands, such as Lucky Fox, Steel Blues, and the co-ed Blue Jean, were mostly content to play cover versions of Western hits like the inescapable "Hotel California," seemingly Taiwan's unofficial national anthem.

Little more than a year after armed police had driven Lost Week-end from Dirty Roger's stage, there were now plenty of opportunities to play music in public, largely owing to the foreign musicians' persistent efforts to establish a live performance circuit. Misery, as well as various ad-hoc expat groups such as the Claydermen (a wry nod to Richard) and the free-improvising Cyberspace Chamber of Commerce (a collaboration between Jazz Cowboys' George Soler and past and present members of Identity Crisis), regularly shared bills with Taiwanese bands at pubs, cafés, the university, and on the grounds of the Tainan Cultural Center. It looked like a vibrant little scene was taking root in the unlikely soil of Tainan after all.

Expatriate musical activity continued to flourish until the end of the year, when the police suddenly began raiding clubs and deporting foreign musicians with a vengeance. For years, Taiwanese offi-fficials had turned a blind eye on the hundreds of foreigners—mostly Filipinos but also including a few dozen Westerners—who played in nightclubs and piano lounges from Taipei to Kaohsiung. Although it was technically illegal for foreign nationals to work without a permit in Taiwan, the authorities had long been lax in enforcing the law, hence the small army of transient English teachers working in the island's larger cities. While the purge of unauthorized foreign work-ers eventually did extend to English teachers as well, musicians were the first to be singled out for harassment. Some speculated that the raids came in response to complaints from Taiwanese musicians that foreigners were putting them out of work; more likely, the government simply felt that itinerant foreign musicians were undesirables.

Among the victims of the crackdown was my Identity Crisis comrade Andreas Vath. Some months before the sweep, the long-haired bassist had taken a gig accompanying lounge pianists at a classy Tainan nightclub to supplement his student stipend. The engagement proved lucrative until the cops made a surprise visit to the club one evening when Andreas was on stage. Caught like the proverbial deer in the headlights, he was promptly escorted to the local precinct house and forced to surrender his student visa. After receiving a lecture on Taiwanese employment law, he asked the officer in charge if he would be allowed to resume his studies and was assured that he could do so by simply reapplying for a student visa at a Taiwan consular office anywhere outside the country. The next day Andreas dutifully flew to Seoul and obtained a new student visa without incident. Confident that he'd put his troubles behind him, he flew back to Taiwan the following day—and was flatly denied entrance by customs officers, who declared his student visa invalid. Fortunately, he had just enough money on his person to fly home to Germany, but his musical instruments and other belongings remained in Tainan. Back in Germany, Andreas repeatedly petitioned the ROC government for permission to continue his language studies in Taiwan but was turned down cold, an unreasonably harsh punishment for such an innocuous transgression. Two years later he was finally granted a one-week visa for the sole purpose of collecting his property. Several more years passed before he was finally cleared to travel to Taiwan without restriction.

Friends in Taipei alerted us that the police were targeting expat musicians in that city as well, in some cases actually whisking players offstage and taking them straight to the airport for deportation. The draconian new policy delivered a devastating blow to businesses like the Feelmore Jazz Pub, which had relied on foreign acts to draw customers. After a year of presenting expat bands to full houses, the Feelmore closed for good shortly after the crackdown.

Unlike many foreign musicians in Taiwan, I never accepted an engagement just to make a buck. Sure, I did make a little pocket money now and then, but nothing to compare with the high wages routinely earned by English teachers. More often than not, my bands lost money on gigs after the cost of equipment, rehearsal room rental, and transportation was factored in. In Taiwan, as in any other place, playing noncommercial music simply doesn't pay. However, this didn't prevent me from coming in for my share of police harassment.

Since my return from China the previous year, it had grown noticeably more difficult to renew my visa every two months, as required by the ROC government. As the husband of a full-time student, I was supposedly entitled by law to stay for as long as Anne's student visa remained valid, but the police were clearly suspicious of my purposes and had started asking questions about my musical involvements, implying that I was working illegally. Of course, I *was* working illegally, but as an English teacher, not a musician; it was far more remunerative.

One afternoon, the police made an unannounced visit to my apartment to confront me about my music-making. Fortunately I wasn't home at the time, but I now realized that a showdown with the authorities was inevitable. Suspicious as to why the cops had tracked me down at my residence, I did some investigating and found out that our nemesis Mrs. Guo, the owner of the skin-care salon next door, had snitched on me. Apparently the police had come down on her for violating some regulation about hanging commercial signs over the sidewalk. Hoping to deflect attention from herself and drive out her despised foreign neighbors in the bargain, she eagerly blew the whistle on the American musician next door.

In view of what had happened to Andreas, I started packing my bags in anticipation of being deported. Providentially, Anne had a loyal student whose father was well connected in local power circles and willing to intervene on my behalf. Mr. Tseng obligingly contacted a crony on the police force and successfully argued my case, though I still had to submit to a grilling at the local precinct house. I was rather taken aback to learn that the police had been following my musical exploits in the pages of *Modern Times*, which often reported on my shows. I patiently explained to my interrogators that I viewed my concerts as a public service because they actually cost me money, but they obviously thought I was trying to bullshit them. In their view, there was no point in playing music unless there was a profit to be made, an attitude that is sadly prevalent the world over. In the end, Anne's *guanxi*—the network of connections and mutual obligations that is central to Chinese culture—spared me deportation, but I was deeply disheartened that the authorities had so completely misunderstood my efforts to promote meaningful cultural exchange. To emphasize my good intentions, I explicitly described all my subsequent shows as nonprofit events, or "no wage" music as one concert poster put it.

I experienced yet another setback when the Identity Crisis CD for Crystal Records fell through. Upon returning from the Vagaries' China tour I had contacted label boss A-Da Im and scheduled a second studio session for the purpose of touching up a few songs and mixing the tapes for release. By this time three of the four musicians who'd played on the initial recording session had left Taiwan, so I recruited two new collaborators: former Gang of Formosa member Volker Wiedersheim and newly arrived Canadian-American multi-instrumentalist Matthew Clark, who some years later would become Cui Jian's international manager and produce the finest compilation of Mainland Chinese rock music I've heard to date.

On the agreed-upon date I flew to Taipei with Matt and a very shaky Volker, who had just been discharged from a Tainan hospital after a severe bout of hepatitis. To our great annoyance, our appearance at Crystal's offices caught A-Da completely by surprise; he had never scheduled the promised studio session and tried to cover his ass by claiming that he'd only meant to meet with us to discuss the project's future. I erupted, flabbergasted at his incompetence. Had we flown all the way to bloody Taipei with our gear and the ailing Volker just to be casually put off?

My tirade had the desired effect, as a browbeaten A-Da reluctantly telephoned a recording studio and booked time for the following day. Once in the studio, we enjoyed a productive session under the direction of a recording engineer who went by the curious name of Birdy, yet it was growing obvious that A-Da had lost interest in the Identity Crisis project. Not without justification, he complained that the drum tracks were too erratic and impossible to correct without starting all over again. Unfortunately, our erstwhile record producer, George Soler, wasn't there to lobby on our behalf, having had a serious falling-out with A-Da in the interim, so the project was simply scrapped, to the band's lasting disappointment. All we had to show for our efforts was Matt's permanent hearing impairment after singing his lungs out with a hole in his eardrum.

With the session now out of the way, it became clear that A-Da's real purpose in courting Identity Crisis was to leverage my connections in hopes of recruiting rising mainland Chinese musicians to the Crystal Records roster. A number of Taiwanese record labels were already looking west to the motherland for fresh talent at bargain prices, and A-Da was transparently hungry for a piece of the action. Hoping to exploit my access to Cui Jian and other mainland rockers, the obsequious label boss invited me to join him and Birdy on a talent-scouting mission to Beijing. I mulled it over momentarily but politely declined, reluctant to bear the onus of hooking my friends up with a record industry shyster.

Identity Crisis wasn't the only act to get burned by Crystal Records. Label mainstays Chen Ming-chang and Sissy flew the coop around this time over financial conflicts, George Soler never received fair compensation for long hours of production work, and the Jazz Cowboys eventually discovered that their CD sales had been vastly underreported. The company sputtered on for a few more years as an importer of foreign records before being absorbed into a media conglomerate. It depressed me to realize that even an outwardly idealistic record label like Crystal, with its indispensable catalog of modern Taiwanese music, was just like all the others in the end.

Though music was the thread that connected my experiences in Taiwan, other aspects of life on the island also left powerful and sometimes painful memories. Most disturbing were my several close brushes with appalling violence.

In class discussions, my adult students would universally denounce the United States as a violent, gun-loving society, and they got no argument from me. Yet though I have hitchhiked all over the U.S. and lived in some extremely grim sections of New York City, to this day I've never encountered as much foul play as I did in my three short years in Taiwan. Kidnapping, burglary, extortion, and underworld violence were commonplace at the time, and it wasn't long before such ugly incidents struck uncomfortably close to home. The first crime involved two of our adolescent English students at the elite language school Mama Hu's. The children's family lived above the jewelry store they owned in the city center. One night burglars broke into the home through an upstairs window, bent on making off with valuables stashed inside a heavy safe. The thieves rolled up the boys' mother in a rug where she suffocated to death, then nearly sawed off the father's hands to force him to divulge the safe combination. Incredibly, both children were back in our English classes the next day.

Soon after this brutal episode, an even more gruesome fate befell an acquaintance's brother, the owner of a basement bar frequented by a disreputable crowd. One night after closing time, as the owner and his friends partied unawares over a card game, a gangster pulled up outside, poured several liters of gasoline through a gap in the security door, and set it aflame, roasting the trapped occupants to death. In a brazen parting flourish, the perpetrator torched a dozen parked motorcycles before riding away.

Most heartbreaking of all was the tragic tale of Andrew, a six-year-old kindergarten student at the language school where Anne and I taught every morning. Andrew stood out from his classmates on account of his irrepressibly unruly behavior and suspicious proclivity for getting banged up. The kid was a real handful in class, but one couldn't help liking him, with his easy laughter and mischievous glint in the eye. Over the course of the semester we noticed that Andrew was showing up for class with one injury after another. With mounting alarm, we observed that his injuries were steadily worsening, from the occasional black eye or bandaged boo-boo to a broken arm and a constellation of black and blue bumps on his visibly misshapen head. The Taiwanese teaching assistants made lame attempts to deny this obvious case of runaway parental abuse by claiming that Andrew had "hurt himself," but we weren't buying it. Rumor had it that Andrew's parentage was in doubt and that the shamed father consequently missed no opportunity to vent his rage on the blameless child. Filled with foreboding, Anne and I urged school officials to intervene while there was still time, but while they were plainly troubled by Andrew's plight, they instead chose to respect the Chinese father's inviolable right to do as he wishes with his child.

The outcome was all too predictable. One morning I walked into my kindergarten classroom to find all the kids in a state of high excitement. One of the little girls suddenly blurted out, "Teacher! Teacher! Andrew's dead!" My stomach flip-flopped. A teaching assistant quickly appeared and explained that Andrew had "fallen down the stairs at home," but her eyes told a different story. Stunned speechless, I filled with rage over the snuffing of this young life. In recent weeks I had begun to form a bond with the wayward boy, who'd started to make good progress in class. What made Andrew's murder especially galling was that it could so easily have been prevented were it not for the rigidity of traditional familial mores. Several school officials privately demanded an inquiry, but the father naturally got off scot-free.

And these weren't isolated incidents. A Canadian teacher was kidnapped from an expatriate bar by gangsters, taken for a joy ride with a pistol barrel in his mouth, and then forced to kneel in a field with his back to his abductors. Determined not to die in such a sordid manner, he ran for all he was worth and managed to escape. Around the same time a young American woman was drugged by her adult English student at his family's teahouse and awoke hours later in a groggy stupor to find that she'd been raped. And in another harrowing scene, a large party of foreigners was drinking beer at a Tainan pub when a vicious fight suddenly broke out among some small-time hoodlums at the next table. In a flash, one of the combatants leapt up, smashed his beer mug on the edge of the table and slashed his opponent with the jagged edge, leaving the astonished victim's finger half-severed. Everyone at our table froze in silence except Anne, who mortified me by rushing over to berate the fighters. Certain that I would be drawn into a bloody fracas to defend my Good Samaritan wife, I saw my life start to unspool before my eyes, but Anne's righteous outburst miraculously stopped the startled belligerents in their tracks. Fortunately, despite all this exposure to violence, we were never victimized personally (except for the time I got slugged in the chest by a ruffian for mouthing off), but such incidents betrayed tightly wound tensions that lay just beneath the surface of what was outwardly a very mannered and orderly society.

After three years of playing for a core audience of expatriates, I had grown frustrated at my seeming failure to cultivate an appreciative audience among the Taiwanese—quite the opposite of my experience in China, where my audiences were almost entirely Chinese. Granted, the music my bands played was both unfashionable and unfamiliar, but the many jazz CDs on display in Tainan record shops gave evidence that a potential audience for our music did exist. It gradually dawned on me that the problem might not be the type of music we played so much as where we played it. Most Taiwanese were justifiably uncomfortable listening to music in loud, smoky bars frequented by drunken foreigners. There was also a widespread assumption that music played in such establishments was not "serious," and skeptics wondered why, if we were such good musicians, we were playing in dives and studying Chinese in provincial Tainan. They certainly had a point. Perhaps more people would take our music seriously if we presented it at a legitimate performance venue.

In the summer of 1992, Tainan's first contemporary arts center, the New Phase Art Space, opened in an attractive downtown loca-tion. Equipped with a minimalist "black box" performance space for concerts, lectures, and films, the New Phase seemed an ideal venue in which to test my theory that a change in our presentation strat-egy would draw more listeners. I succeeded in setting up a con-cert at the New Phase through contacts in the city's art scene and assembled a six-piece group named Axolotl (after a peculiar sala-mander species) for the occasion. The band was made up of vet-erans Mark DeForge and Matthew Clark,

Program for Axolotl concert at New Phase Art Space, Tainan, Taiwan, 1992. L-R: Mark DeForge, Ryan Berg, Matthew Corbin Clark, Alex Crane, Dennis Rea, Axel Schunn

plus recent arrivals Ryan Berg from California (on bass), Alex Crane from Toronto (on keyboards), and Axel Schunn from Berlin (on guitar). In an effort to break with our bar band image, we planned an ambitious program complete with performance art, video, and projected images and rehearsed exhaustively for weeks. For their part, the New Phase staff hyped the show heavily in the gallery's calendar and newsletter.

Tickets sold out quickly and, as I'd hoped, the concert attracted a greater number of Taiwanese than usual. Regrettably, however, on this occasion our reach definitely exceeded our grasp. Several of our ambitious multimedia experiments went seriously awry: An attempt to improvise musical interpretations of noted painter Lin Hong-Wen's projected artworks faltered badly because of almost comical miscommunication, and Mark DeForge's performance—wrapped as a mummy against a backdrop of video images of the recent Los Angeles riots—left many in the audience feeling a bit rattled. Despite the large turnout and charitably warm response, the Axolotl concert failed to live up to our lofty ambitions.

Toward the end of 1992, Anne and I finally made the oft-postponed decision to move back to the States after nearly half a decade abroad. By this time we had both secured resident visas that allowed us to work indefinitely in Taiwan, but we had a growing sense that if we didn't pick up the threads of our former lives in Seattle soon, we would risk becoming permanent expatriates, like many of our American and European friends who remain comfortably ensconced in Tainan to this day. Though it would have been easy to continue teaching English part time and forming ad-hoc bands with whomever happened to pass through town, I increasingly felt a need to measure the rich and rewarding experiences of my sojourn abroad against the realities of my own culture, and to reconnect with the friends and family members I'd left behind.

I resolved to devote my remaining two months in Taiwan to making one final effort to stage the high-caliber musical event I had long envisioned. Once again I scheduled a concert at the New Phase Art Space, this time featuring a motley assemblage under the name the Lemming Dynasty, a lame pun on China's Ming Dynasty. This was the largest, most culturally integrated group I had yet worked with overseas, comprising four Americans (me, Ryan Berg, violinist Charles Estus, and percussionist Dave Treanor), two Canadians (Alex Crane and Matt Clark), a German (Axel Schunn), and a Tainan native (former Identity Crisis drummer Tsao Hsin, just back from an extended stay in England). Together we conceived a kaleidoscopic program spanning jazz, reggae, Gypsy music, bossa nova, cowboy twang, percussion workouts, computer music, Spanish-and African-flavored pieces, and classic tunes by the likes of Bill Evans and Henry Mancini.

Drawing a lesson from Axolotl's embarrassing technical hiccups, the Lemming Dynasty chose to dispense with the theatrics and focus entirely on the music. Much to my delight, the resulting concert, again heavily attended by Taiwanese, was easily the most satisfying musical experience of my tenure in Taiwan. A fortuitous confluence of circumstance, hard work, and good intent brought about one of those rare instances of musical *satori* to which all musicians aspire—when the muse takes the players into her embrace, inspiration flows unimpeded, and genuine communication takes place between audience and performers. This is really what it's all about in the end. Best of all, the audience demonstrably loved the music, applauding generously and laughing out loud at the occasional odd sound effect. After the show, several attendees remarked with surprise that they had never realized we were such talented musicians.

A few days later our landlady, Mrs. Huang, told me that her 80-year-old mother was still raving about the Lemming Dynasty concert. The realization that our music had touched this woman across daunting cultural, linguistic, and generational barriers was the ultimate affirmation of my endeavors in China and Taiwan. I could now return home knowing that all the struggles and frustrations of the past four years—the equipment failures, lying promoters, police hassles, shady record deals, and misunderstandings—had not been in vain.

For all I knew at the time, the Lemming Dynasty concert would be my last performance in the Far East. It meant the world to me that this chapter of my life had closed on such a high note. Now it was time to go home, absorb my life-changing experiences, and adapt myself to what had become a completely alien world.

# CHAPTER 20

# THE OTHER FOOT

Anne and I moved back to Seattle in February 1993, more than four years after we'd migrated overseas for an expected year of teaching English. Bill Clinton had just been sworn in to office, ushering in a decade of dot-com excess and illusory post–Cold War euphoria. Thankfully, we had missed the entire presidency of the sinister Bush I.

After such a long spell outside the country, reverse culture shock set in rapidly and left us feeling like strangers in our own culture. For months we struggled to reorient ourselves, searching fruitlessly for meaningful jobs while our savings from Taiwan steadily dwindled. We had come home confident that we could parlay our teaching experience into paying jobs as ESL instructors in Seattle's sizable immigrant community, but we soon discovered that Americans with similar teaching credentials were commonplace in the Puget Sound area. Anne went back to school to earn her master's degree and eventually became an English professor, while I ended up taking a "permatemp" gig as a writer and editor at Microsoft like so many other Seattle residents who possessed a modicum of literary skill.

To my lasting amazement, the insular Seattle music scene that I'd abandoned for the uncertainties of China had exploded into the international limelight while we were abroad. A half-dozen Northwest rock bands, led by Nirvana, Pearl Jam, and Soundgarden, had risen to dominate the global music charts and would soon project their influence even into China. In a few short years the grunge-rock revolution, which was just getting off the ground when I left in

1989, had transformed the city into a place of pilgrimage for hordes of aspiring rockers and hangers-on. Back in 1989 there were only three music venues in all of Seattle that booked original local bands; now there were 30 or 40. One estimate put the number of rock groups in Seattle at more than 2,000, meaning that roughly one out of every 10 Seattleites played in a band.

As the 1990s wore on, many members of the flannel-shirt fraternity outgrew grunge and became involved in more forward-looking genres such as modern jazz, free improvisation, and electronic music. Once-marginal musical styles began to flourish, attracting accomplished musicians to Seattle in ever-greater numbers. After years of isolation as a progressive musician in the Far East, I was now surrounded by ferociously talented players who challenged me to take my music to the next level. Yet while I did find plenty of opportunities to play music in public, after the highs I'd experienced gigging in the Far East, the prosaic workaday reality of Seattle was a crashing comedown.

China seemed far away indeed when I received the improbable news that Cui Jian was scheduled to appear at Seattle's annual Bumbershoot arts festival in September 1994. The elder statesman of Chinese rock was not only coming to the U.S., but to the city where I lived! Who would have imagined that Cui Jian would one day undergo the mirror image of my own experience in China?

A sprawling four-day event held every Labor Day weekend, Bumbershoot (a synonym for "umbrella") features hundreds of international, national, and local artists on more than a dozen stages in the shadow of the Space Needle. With its reputation for globe-spanning eclecticism, the festival seemed a highly appropriate forum for a rock star hailing from the alluring East. That year's edition of the festival even had a Chinese theme, with featured appearances by several notable Chinese authors in addition to Cui Jian. I was impressed that the organizers had successfully secured the Chinese government's permission to present an artist who posed such a political liability, a scenario that would have been unimaginable just a few years earlier. Had Beijing decided that, in the blasé '90s, Cui Jian no longer posed much of a threat, or had they correctly surmised that few Americans would even take note of the singer's presence?

With Cui Jian's U.S. debut, one of rock music's more unusual offshoots had come full circle. Although he had previously performed abroad in Europe, Japan, and Hong Kong, his arrival in the birthplace of rock and roll represented a musical homecoming of sorts. Regrettably, the significance of his visit was lost on most of the listening public. The Seattle media provided only cursory coverage of the event, focusing almost exclusively on the singer's tenuous link to the 1989 events at Tiananmen Square while ignoring the broader implications of his role as a barrier-breaking creative artist and exemplar for China's disaffected younger generation.

Cui Jian's visit came on the heels of the release of his latest album, the provocatively titled *Balls under the Red Flag*. Musically, *Balls* was his most radical departure to date from the stirring ballads that had inspired Chinese youth in the 1980s. With its harsh textures and insistent dissonance, *Balls* seemed almost calculated to alienate Cui Jian's longtime admirers. The new album balanced a more contemporary, musically aware approach—postmodern musical irony, an industrial oil-barrel drum kit, blasts of twisted free jazz—with a renewed emphasis on native instruments like the double-reed *suona*. The record also reunited Cui Jian with guitarist Eddie Randriama Pionona and saxophonist Liu Yuan, his former bandmates in the pioneering group ADO.

Lao Cui's ("Old Cui") long-awaited U.S. debut proved disappointingly anticlimactic thanks to poor strategic decisions on the part of festival organizers. A free event for many years, Bumbershoot had recently come under fire for instituting an admission fee. In an attempt to placate critics who felt the festival was becoming too commercial, organizers announced that the first day, a Friday, would be free. But there was a catch: Five of Friday's most attractive acts, including Cui Jian, were lumped together as an event-within-an-event that carried a separate admission fee. Given a choice between dozens of free musical acts or five bands at a price, most concertgoers understandably opted for the former. So when the Beijing rockers took the stage for an ill-timed 5 P.M. concert, they found themselves playing to fewer than 100 people—in a football stadium, no less. Despite this disheartening reception, the band delivered their set with dignity and energy. Bumbershoot officials shrugged off the flop, calling it a "warm-up" for a second show slated for Sunday.

That evening at a party for Cui Jian hosted by the former Vagaries, several of his band members expressed interest in having an informal jam with Seattle musicians. Photographer Spike Mafford made some calls and succeeded in arranging an after-hours encounter at MOE, the city's trendiest rock club at the time. Cui Jian and his group showed up at MOE expecting a casual jam session, only to find the house packed with local scenesters who'd been promised a "surprise guest" by the excited club owners—rather like Identity Crisis' experience at the Citli All-Night Club gathering in Beijing. The Chinese musicians visibly brightened upon entering the room—it was clear that they'd been hoping for a genuine rock club experience in the U.S. rather than the overly formal arena events planned by Bumbershoot organizers, much as the Vagaries had preferred underground gigs to the confining straitjacket of the Sichuan-China International TV Festival.

After a brief introduction, Cui Jian, Eddie, Liu Yuan, and bassist Zhang Ling took the stage, joined by drummer Jason Finn of the hugely popular Presidents of the United States of America, who'd been recruited just moments before the show. The band jumped right into a bracing version of Cui Jian's quasi-rap number "Solution," with Finn doing an impressive job of handling the unfamiliar material behind the kit. Though the audience had never even heard of Cui Jian, they roared in approval, and the visiting musicians were clearly inspired by their first taste of the U.S. club scene. The surprise set concluded with the title song from *Balls under the Red Flag*, augmented by violinist Eyvind Kang and me on guitar. The tune evolved into a wide-ranging, funky improvisation that continued until the club shut down at 2 A.M.

Looking back on Cui Jian's appearance at MOE, I can't help but savor the irony of grunge-generation American scenesters happily gyrating to *Balls under the Red Flag*'s chorus:

> *The Red Flag is still waving,*
> *But now without direction.*
> *The Revolution rolls on.*
> *The Old Man is stronger.*

As critic Jon Pareles later wrote in an article about the singer in the *New York Times*, "Unlike the Western grunge rockers, Cui Jian sings about a malaise that is not self-induced."

Cui Jian's second Bumbershoot concert more than made up for the football stadium fiasco. Close to 1,000 people attended the show at the genteel Opera House, including a sizable contingent from Seattle's Chinese community. Others came from as far away as Vancouver and California to see China's rock and roll legend. At length Cui Jian walked on stage to a chorus of cheers in English, Mandarin, and Cantonese. The band played most of *Balls* and a few numbers from *Solution*, saving the classic "Yi Wu Suo You" for last. (At one point Cui Jian confessed to me that he would gladly never play the much-requested song again.) During his rendition of "The Other Shore," Cui Jian assumed the role of musical diplomat, improvising English lyrics calling for better understanding between our respective cultures. The applause was loud and long. The band's focused and powerful performance was marred only by its brevity, the result of an overlong opening set by a Seattle rock band. Afterwards, Cui Jian seemed genuinely touched at being mobbed by a throng of Chinese-American autograph seekers.

For those in the audience who'd experienced a Cui Jian performance in China, it was like being teleported back to the motherland, with wildly excited Chinese fans shouting and singing along. Newcomers to his music were likewise swept up in the surge of emotion. Many in the audience, including the manager of grunge titans Soundgarden and Alice in Chains, remarked that the music possessed a vitality that had all but disappeared from corporate Western rock.

On his final night in Seattle, Cui Jian told filmmaker Lisa Dutton that his experience in America had left him feeling like a "real musician." This might seem a curious remark coming from someone who'd single-handedly revolutionized popular music in the world's most populous nation, but in the rock clubs of ultra-hip Seattle, where few knew or cared who he was, Cui Jian had finally succeeded in winning over listeners on the merits of his music rather than his politics.

A year later Cui Jian again crossed the Pacific for his first multi-city U.S. tour, including dates in San Francisco, New York, Boston, and… Kalamazoo, Michigan? I couldn't fathom why he had booked a show in this sleepy Midwestern city of 80,000 people, but it turned out that Kalamazoo was the hometown of his Chinese-American girlfriend, Ann.

By odd coincidence, I was in Michigan at the same time visiting my own Anne, who was finishing up graduate school not far from Kalamazoo. I drove to the city with onetime Lemming Dynasty violinist Charles Estus and caught the end of the band's set at a downtown rock dive named Club Soda, where they were playing for about 150 spectators in an outdoor beer garden. The fans— mostly Chinese university students—were beside themselves with excitement, dancing and clapping and singing along with his better-known tunes. After the show Chinese autograph hounds approached the singer with deferential awe. I spent about an hour with the Cui Jian and his musicians, who were very surprised to see me so far from Seattle, before they left on a red-eye flight to their next stop, New York.

Cui Jian was a big hit in New York, where he played three engagements at the Palladium, the Bottom Line, and downtown avant-music shrine the Knitting Factory. Of the three shows, the Palladium concert was the best attended, with about 2,000 mostly Chinese audience members on hand. Even the Chinese diplomatic corps were spotted in the crowd. In a subsequent concert review, the *Village Voice* wrote, "If, in America, Chinese people have a reputation for being staid, this was the concert to break the stereotype... the room was electric with excitement." On a more critical note, the *Voice* observed that "this international rock star's tendency is to weave in so many influences that the thread gets lost. Cui Jian's songs work best when he blends them with Beijing style and flavor, making them distinctly his own."

When asked what he thought of the Big Apple, Cui Jian told the *New York Times* that he felt like "a fish that had finally found water" and described the city as "heaven for music." Yet after two trips to the U.S., Cui Jian still hadn't succeeded in breaking through to non-Chinese listeners. It would be logical to presume that this was due to the language barrier, for Cui Jian's songs otherwise compared favorably with much currently fashionable international pop and rock; but then how does one explain the perennial popularity of African and Brazilian music in urban America? A more likely explanation is simply that Cui Jian's music is largely unavailable in the West and that his tour organizers made little effort to promote him to an American audience.

China's all-woman rock band Cobra fared considerably worse than Cui Jian on their own visit to the United States in 1996. The group traveled to the U.S. at the instigation of Victor Huey, a New York–based documentary filmmaker and longtime chronicler of the Chinese music scene. At their first Stateside appearance as part of the gender-segregated Michigan Womyn's Festival, the Chinese women were taken aback at the sight of bare-breasted concertgoers dancing in the aisles, confirming their suspicions of American depravity. The band went on to play shows in New York clubs Wetlands and CBGBs, where their retro–New Wave stylings, heavily influenced by 1980s bands like the Cure, fell flat on the jaded downtown crowd. *New York Times* critic Jon Pareles voiced disappointment at the lack of identifiably Chinese elements in the band's music, complaining that the group never really "cut loose," an observation echoed by former Identity Crisis/Axolotl member Matthew Corbin Clark, who operated the sound board at one of the group's New York shows. Matt added that, unlike Cui Jian and his band, the members of Cobra showed little interest in their surroundings, rarely ventured outside the apartment of a friend in Chinatown, and were highly critical of all things American. Accustomed to being treated like "stars" in inbred Beijing rock circles, Cobra found their exposure to the big-league New York music scene a cold shower.

These first tentative forays into the international musical marketplace raise doubts as to whether Chinese musicians will ever catch on with a global audience. Despite the explosion of interest in world music, Western listeners have thus far shown a marked preference for Afro-Caribbean musical styles characterized by sunny melodies and danceable rhythms. Some might argue that there really is an impenetrable "great wall of sound" separating China from other musical cultures, yet all bets are off as Chinese musicians continue to experiment and absorb musical input from around the increasingly interconnected globe.

One memorable incident gave me hope that any real or imagined musical differences can eventually be bridged. In 1999, Cui Jian and his band returned to Seattle to play the gigantic World of Music and Dance (WOMAD) Festival alongside leading musicians from around the planet. (I had the honor of joining him on stage for the all-star festival wind-up, alongside the likes of Joan Baez and the master drummers of Burundi.) After the festival wound down, CJ expressed interest in checking out the Seattle club scene, so I took him to downtown nightspot the 700 Club, which hosted a fashionable hip-hop and funk scene. We arrived to find an open-mic session in progress, with wannabe rappers taking turns showing off their stuff to the accompaniment of house musicians. On a dare from his band members, an initially shy Cui Jian agreed to take a crack at rapping. Introduced simply as "CJ from Beijing," Cui Jian and his young drummer, Bebe, proceeded to stun the crowd with a rapid-fire, double-barrel display of virtuosic Chinese wordplay. (The Chinese lexicon of single-syllable words lends itself surprisingly well to rapping.) Excited clubgoers crowded around the stage and whooped with delight, much as I'd witnessed at underground rock shows in China. CJ won the night's contest hands-down, and not a soul present except his friends had any idea that he was the most famous musician in the largest country in the world.

**96**

北京国际 Jazz 爵士乐集萃

**Beijing International Jazz Festival**

主办：北京伊人文化交流艺术中心
承办：北京环球文化交流服务公司
协办：中国国际广播电台·英语台 91.5、
　　　北京环球文化旅行社

感谢北京市伊人广告公司特别赞助

Organizer: Beijing Yiren Culture & Arts Exchange Center
Co-Organizer: Beijing World Culture Exchange Service Co.
Co-Sponsor: China Radio International, English Service 91.5FM,
　　　　Beijing World Cultural Travel Service

Special Thanks to Beijing Yiren Advertising Company

# EPILOGUE

# INNOCENCE LOST

It's November 1996 and I'm back in Chengdu, the city where my improbable cross-cultural musical odyssey began eight years earlier. This time I'm here with Land, a Seattle-based instrumental sextet that purveys an odd blend of jazz, rock, electronic, and world music, easily the strangest offering I've yet foisted on unsuspecting Chinese audiences. Fittingly, Land includes my former collaborator from the Taiwan days, George Soler, to whom I've finally made good on my promise of a China tour. The other members of Land are well-known experimental composer and keyboardist Jeff Greinke, acclaimed trumpet improviser Lesli Dalaba, and dual percussionists Greg Gilmore and Bill Moyer.

So far our tour has taken us to the highbrow Beijing International Jazz Festival, an avant-garde arts center in Hong Kong, a Portuguese cultural festival in Macau's architecturally stunning public square, and a swank music club in no-longer-provincial Kunming, where dozens of rock bands influenced by Cui Jian and Seattle grunge have formed in the five short years since the Vagaries played the city's first-ever public rock concert—and where a huge Wal-Mart now does a thriving business.

In stark contrast to the punishing, technologically challenged, and financially disastrous Identity Crisis and Vagaries tours, we've been incredibly pampered on this outing, sleeping in posh four-star hotels every night and flying from city to city at our hosts' expense. The sound equipment at venues has been top-notch—this time an amp really *is* an amp—and wonder of wonders, we're actually *making* money. Gone are the days of playing for dirt-poor students in frozen classrooms and rinky-dink discos; on this tour we're entertaining audiences of fat-cat businessmen and upwardly mobile urban sophisticates at venues like the brand-new Rhinoceros Garden resort outside Chengdu, a strikingly bourgeois recreational complex complete with a golf course, tennis courts, and all manner of upscale amenities.

Throughout the tour I've been continually amazed at the wholesale transformation of China, but it comes as a real shock to find my old home base of Chengdu transfigured, or perhaps more accurately disfigured, almost beyond recognition. Like every other city in China, Sichuan's capital has been radically reshaped by relentless development and all its attendant traffic and environmental woes. In just seven years, entire neighborhoods of historic narrow lanes and timbered houses have been razed to clear space for a forest of gaudy skyscrapers, and miles of the surrounding paddy country have been eaten up by runaway construction. Where mom-and-pop noodle stalls once lined the dusty streets, high-class restaurants, luxury hotel towers, karaoke palaces, and even microbrew pubs are now ubiquitous; where I once pedaled my bicycle around at a leisurely pace, a roaring torrent of automobiles now races day and night. The disappearance of the Chengdu I knew and loved deeply depresses me, but I wonder if my indulgence in nostalgia is mere selfishness, for my old friends are all better off materially than ever before. Who am I to begrudge them the comforts of modernity?

The city's newfound prosperity has also brought a startling leap in musical sophistication. I would never have imagined in 1989 that just a few years later I would be able to purchase a Chinese translation of John Cage's revolutionary treatise "The Future of Music" in a Chengdu bookstore; that a newly established Sichuan Modern Pop Music Institute (under the direction of my former record producer Yang Shichun) would enroll hundreds of students eager to study jazz and electronic music; or that a reggae bar would become popular with a hip young clientele. A nationally influential rock music scene is in full bloom, and the city's first jazz club is set to open this week with an inaugural performance by members of Land. One foreign journalist has gone so far as to gush that "a remarkable youth culture scene is flowering in the remote western Chinese city of Chengdu, where punk, grunge, and performance artists perform to their own, distinctive beat… the city's art and music scene has a verve and life which can rival China's capital Beijing or wealthy Shanghai." I can hardly believe how much progress the city's music community, and China's in general, has made in such a brief time span. Or has it?

Back in 1991 when Identity Crisis played in Beijing, it was not unreasonable to hope that a vanguard of visionary rock musicians would help effect a transformation of Chinese society. Conditions were ripe for change in a nation whose citizens were thoroughly jaded with hypocritical Communist rhetoric and outraged over institutionalized corruption and the butchery at Tiananmen.

Seeking to deflect attention from his country's deepening political crisis, in 1992 Deng Xiaoping had publicly reaffirmed his conviction that "to get rich is glorious," igniting a sweeping entrepreneurial revolution that quickly transformed China into the world's fastest growing economy. Privately owned shops and restaurants sprang up everywhere like mushrooms after a spring squall. Consumer goods proliferated, the country's first stock exchange opened for business, and moribund state enterprises and even the military expanded their activities into real estate and commerce. Deng's strategy neatly defused a volatile political predicament in the bargain, for with fortunes waiting to be made on China's surging economic roller coaster, most Chinese would rather get a piece of the action than risk their necks for democratic ideals.

Ironically, the perennially marginalized rock scene was also swept up in the boomtown mentality. China's recording industry, long a strictly controlled government monopoly, rapidly became an arena of capitalist enterprise. Homegrown rock crept out of its furtive subculture of secret parties and embassy events and onto the stages of commercial rock clubs and flashy international franchises like the Hard Rock Café, now tolerated as legitimate moneymaking ventures. Onetime *bête noir* Cui Jian was once again allowed to perform throughout the motherland and even made multiple tours of Europe and the U.S. But by far the most fateful development was the invasion of China by multinational music conglomerates and MTV, which forever changed the face of Chinese music.

Soon after satellite networks like Hong Kong's Star TV began beaming previously *verboten* international programming into Chinese homes in the early 1990s, a new generation of MTV-influenced rock bands rose to prominence, led by the hirsute Tang Dynasty, power-pop heartthrobs Black Panther, notorious bad-girl singer "Rose" Luo Qi, and hard rockers Compass (featuring none other than my ambitious young guitarist friend Zhou Di from Chengdu). Many of these groups enjoyed privileges that first-generation Chinese rockers never dreamed of, thanks to hefty transfusions of cash and state-of-the-art equipment from wealthy sponsors in Hong Kong and Taiwan. Yet with few exceptions, most of the second-generation rock bands were content to model themselves after Western acts, and little in their music apart from the lyrics was identifiably Chinese.

Lured by cash advances and the promise of international recognition, the new Beijing bands naïvely signed lopsided contracts with music business predators like Taiwan's Rock Records and Hong Kong's Red Star Productions. Not surprisingly, the labels' glossy production values softened the music's rough edges, robbing it of much of its impact. Worse still, competition for record deals inevitably sowed discord within a music community once distinguished by its solidarity, fomenting jealousy and feuding between rival camps. (In her semi-autobiographical book *Beijing Doll*, author Chun Sue writes that by the late '90s, "everybody hate[d] each other" in the Beijing rock underground.) In sad contrast to the communitarian spirit of early Beijing rock, the scene had become depressingly hierarchical and narcissistic. And even if a band did manage to score a record contract, the rampant piracy endemic to China ensured that they would only see payment for a tiny fraction of the discs and tapes in circulation.

Journalists, business interests, and drug dealers swooped in like carrion fowl to pick the last gobbets off the carcass of the once idealistic Chinese rock scene. The Chinarock phenomenon, as it was now labeled, became the research topic du jour for international China Studies types, prompting a flood of postmodernist theses and documentaries. Beijing musicians found themselves beset by stringers for publications ranging from *Spin* to the *Far Eastern Economic Review* who were eager to scoop an inspiring story about brave rockers defying a repressive communist regime. Meanwhile, corporate sponsorship of rock events spread like a cancer, as in the case of one Beijing rock band that was ordered to play a concert wearing Budweiser T-shirts. And in the grand tradition of Western rock, heroin soon came into vogue among the Beijing rock crowd, leaving a string of senseless casualties in its wake.

Hard on the heels of the second-wave Chinese rockers came the "Peking Punk" movement, typified by amped-up, nihilistic bands with names like Underbaby, Catcher in the Rye, and Brain Failure. Disgusted at their country's headlong slide into materialism, China's punks unfortunately possessed neither the intelligence and compassion of Cui Jian, the novelty shock value of the proto-punk He Yong, nor the musical prowess of Tang Dynasty. For the most part, the music of the Peking Punks was little more than an inarticulate and ultimately impotent tantrum, and remained strictly an underground phenomenon.

But rock music wasn't the only story in 1990s China. Mirroring the proliferation of specialized musical subgenres in the West, Chinese popular music could no longer be split conveniently into *tongsu* (mass music) and *yaogun* (rock) genres—it was now refracted into a bewildering array of styles ranging from rap to techno to death metal. By the end of the decade, Ecstasy-fueled raves were all the rage among an urban youth culture that could barely remember Tiananmen.

Listeners with more refined tastes embraced jazz, which scarcely existed in China back when I delivered my lecture on the genre at Sichuan Music Conservatory in 1989. By the time Land played the Beijing International Jazz Festival in 1996, the four-year-old event was drawing nearly 10,000 listeners for a week of cutting-edge jazz concerts featuring major international artists and a growing number of domestic jazz stars, such as saxophonist Liu Yuan (also a fixture in Cui Jian's band). Similar events soon followed in Shanghai, Hangzhou, and Dalian, while dozens of jazz bars popped up in cities throughout China, sometimes presenting visiting global luminaries such as Wynton Marsalis and Bill Laswell.

One of the more telling musical developments in *fin-de-siècle* China had little, if anything, to do with rock or jazz, namely the advent of Chinese "new age" music. Strangely, the man most responsible for this phenomenon was none other than erstwhile avant-garde composer He Xuntian, who had taken me to task at my lecture years before in Chengdu. After leaving Sichuan in 1992 to join the faculty of the prestigious Shanghai Conservatory of Music, the enterprising He Xuntian struck up a musical partnership with female singer Zhu Zheqin under the name Dadawa. Their collaboration resulted in the massively successful CD *Sister Drum*, a new age spin on Tibetan spiritualism and folk music that became the best-selling recording in Chinese history up to that time and garnered considerable attention in the West. A heavily stylized blend of ersatz Tibetan vocalisms and lush, synthetic backdrops, *Sister Drum* drew heavy criticism from Tibetans, who considered it a patronizing exercise in cultural exoticism that conveniently ignored China's controversial occupation of Tibet.

Interestingly, the sonic bathos typified by *Sister Drum* and its imitators heralded the emergence of a new leisure class in China. Untroubled by the relentless political pogroms of the recent past, and boasting more disposable income than any previous generation,

China's *nouveau riches* could now afford to indulge a taste for the spiritual and the exotic. With its focus on relaxation and a sort of garden-variety spirituality that closely paralleled the Falun Gong pop religion, new age music offered listeners a temporary escape from an increasingly competitive, materialistic lifestyle and a world in which technology and the global marketplace were radically uprooting concepts of nation, culture, and self. In a sense, *Sister Drum* represented a yearning for a mythical golden age in China's past, when poets composed verse leisurely in idyllic riverside pavilions. Seen in this light, it's no wonder that most Chinese listeners preferred the comforting fantasy of *Sister Drum* to the harsh rhythms of Beijing rock.

Happily, a far more promising alternative to either new age vapidity or hard-rock juvenilia was the inception of a germinal community of Chinese improvising musicians in the wake of the Beijing International Jazz Festivals of the mid-1990s. When Land played the 1996 edition of the festival, I was delighted to take part in a series of exhilarating after-hours improvisations hosted by *guzheng* (horizontal zither) virtuoso Wang Yong at his venue Keep in Touch, reputedly the first Internet café in China. Each night, Wang Yong extemporized fluently with a shifting cast of improvisers from around the globe—among them legendary Dutch drummer Han Bennink, American jazz bassist Anthony Cox, British keyboardist Django Bates, and Austrian violinist Andreas Schreiber—showing a remarkable ability to adapt to our widely disparate musical languages. (Wang Yong also joined Land for a subsequent concert in Hong Kong, embroidering our compositions with strikingly complementary *guzheng* solos.) What's more, the packed houses at these late-night gatherings were visibly mesmerized by these demonstrations of unscripted music making. As a musician who's long been passionately involved with free improvisation, I consider the Keep in Touch sessions the most satisfying musical experience of my time in China, as well as the actualization of my long-held wish that Chinese traditional musicians would come forward and improvise on an equal footing with their counterparts from abroad. Though likely to remain a marginal activity at best, free improvisation, with its emphasis on democratic interplay and intent listening, represents the antithesis of the runaway commodity fetishism that marked Chinese popular music at the turn of the century.

The mainstreaming of Chinese rock was a fait accompli by 2002, when Cui Jian's production company staged the much-hyped Snow Mountain Music Festival in Yunnan Province. Dubbed "China's Woodstock" by the international press, the festival attracted thousands of rock fans to a muddy meadow high on the slopes of Jade Dragon Snow Mountain—the very peak I had deliriously trudged around a decade earlier—much to the dismay of local Naxi music historian Xuan Ke, who fretted that the spirit of the sacred mountain would be disturbed by the vulgar sounds of rock and roll. Oblivious to such concerns, longhaired and tattooed rock addicts from all over China drank, danced, and whooped it up in driving rain to the sounds of Cui Jian, Wild Children, Brain Failure, and the cunningly named Confucius Says. Such foreign-influenced debauchery would have been deemed criminal just a few years earlier, but this time the familiar green-uniformed security forces merely looked on in bemusement and tried to dodge the rain. While the event was widely hailed as a great success, Chinese-American rocker Kaiser Kuo observed in *Time* magazine that "Instead of Woodstock innocence, [the festival was marked by] cynical commercialism—by now a defining Chinese characteristic."

Across the Formosa Strait in Taiwan, the tiny creative music scene that my bandmates and I had helped spark in the early 1990s had mushroomed by the end of the decade into Spring Scream, a massive annual open-air rock festival—coincidentally, founded by other Seattle musicians—which draws hordes of audience members to concerts by dozens of local and international bands on multiple stages. In Taipei, huge techno raves take place almost nightly, global avant-garde luminaries like John Zorn fly in regularly to perform concerts of challenging music, and rock megastars like Pearl Jam play to gigantic stadium crowds. On an island where Air Supply was once the epitome of hipness, all-girl Taiwanese punk bands like Ladybug now abuse out-of-tune guitars and scream obscenities at the top of their lungs. Garbage trucks still blare distorted music on the streets of Tainan city, but with a new cosmopolitan twist: Richard Clayderman's puerile piano theme is now overlaid with recorded English lessons, so citizens can enjoy a little "lite" music while practicing their prepositions.

As China and Taiwan move forward into a new millennium in which they will assume an increasingly important role in the global order, will Chinese music finally achieve international prominence befitting a culture that represents a quarter of the world's population? Will creative Chinese artists win the freedom to express themselves without fear of political reprisal? Will the opposing strains of modernism, tradition, and socialism find reconciliation?

With so many political, economic, and social variables hanging in the balance, it seems pointless to make any predictions. But one thing is certain: the Chinese no longer need an obscure, unpedigreed foreign musician like me to open the door to unforeseen musical possibilities. My experience as an unsuspecting emissary of alien music to millions of Chinese can never be repeated in quite the same way, by myself or anyone else. I showed up with guitar in hand at just the right time and place, in the waning days of a period of musical openness and innocence that has since vanished forever in China's headlong rush toward modernity.

As I write this, news arrives that Britney Spears will soon be giving a concert in Beijing.

# AFTERWORD

## TO THE BLUE EAR BOOKS EDITION

A quarter-century after the events that launched this narrative commenced, I find myself in strikingly similar circumstances as I write these lines in the midst of a concert tour of Siberia with a motley assemblage of international musicians. Time and again I'm struck with a sense of *déja vu* as my daily struggles with language, equipment, trying travel conditions, and confounding cultural differences ring all too familiar. How could I have knowingly let myself in for this punishment all over again? As I near the age of 60, the rigors of arduous transcultural travel take a far greater toll on the body and spirit than they did on the wiry, audacious 30-something that was an earlier me. But all the trials and strains dissolve instantly in the smile of a young Buryat musician who's discovering free jazz for the first time, or the lusty shouts of *bravo!* from an elderly *babushka* at a run-down concert hall in Kransk. Despite all the travails of touring, it's become clear that I've deeply missed the sort of transformational experiences that attend to being a musical stranger in a strange land. It is in this state of hazy nostalgia that I cast my eye back on China for the updated Blue Ear Books edition of *Live at the Forbidden City*.

The Siberian cities we're playing, with their dun-colored Soviet-era edifices, shabby infrastructure, and brusque, downcast citizenry, are sometimes remarkably reminiscent of the China I recall. Yet while these Russian backwaters have seemingly remained frozen in time, China—whose northern border lies just a few hundred kilometers distant—has changed nearly beyond recognition in almost every respect. Its hyperventilating economy continues to grow at a dumbfounding pace, minting millionaires by the minute. Gaudy skyscrapers compete with each other to breach the shockingly polluted skies, calling to mind the blooming mineral encrustations of J.G. Ballard's sinister *Crystal World*. Flying Pigeon bicycles have gone the way of the extinct passenger pigeons of yore, supplanted by a monstrous fleet of automobiles contending for every last centimeter of pavement. The scenic and historic Three Gorges of the Yangtze lie entombed beneath a vast artificial lake, while the river's waters are being diverted northward to the Yellow River in a desperate bid to sate an increasingly parched populace. Brand-new "ghost cities" of unoccupied high-rise towers loom at the periphery of China's megalopolises, hedged by rugged badlands of toxic e-waste. Drunk with hubris, the nation's emboldened leaders aggressively stake claim to territories lying far from China's traditional borders, extending even to the moon's surface. An overmatched Taiwan slides meekly into the motherland's cold embrace; uppity Hong Kong will soon exhaust Beijing's parchment-thin tolerance (as evidenced by the latter's response to recent mass protests); and the hated Japanese once again find themselves in the crosshairs of a vengeful Chinese military machine.

Twenty-five years have passed since the infamous events in Tiananmen Square and Chengdu, and still the government has not come clean about its culpability in the spilling of innocent blood. A few outspoken dissidents like Ai Weiwei and Chen Guangcheng continue to be silenced and imprisoned for having the temerity to critique the established order, but they're the rare exceptions in a society that's been largely sapped of revolutionary fervor. Sadly, that goes for the once-defiant Chinese rock scene as well.

I ended the previous edition of *Live at the Forbidden City* on a decidedly downbeat note, observing that "In sad contrast to the communitarian spirit of early Beijing rock, the scene had become depressingly hierarchical and narcissistic." While the rock milieu has grown manyfold since I penned those words, and has even launched a number of notable Chinese bands into the international limelight, little has happened to counter my contention that Chinese rock is largely a spent force in terms of social relevance. As I wrote in 2013, in an essay published in the *Routledge History of Social Protest in Popular Music*:

> Roughly thirty years after rock music first took root in the unlikely ground of communist China, it is difficult to escape the conclusion that it has thus far largely failed to fulfill its promise as a significant force for articulating discontent and effecting meaningful change. Despite its early promise, Chinese rock, to borrow a well-worn Chinese idiom, has largely proven to be a paper tiger ... Perhaps all the hopes pinned on Chinese rock as a political force amount to no more than narcissism, for the West is flattered to see itself reflected in the image of bold Chinese rockers playing "our" music, a sort of reverse-image Cultural Revolution led by guitars and drums.

Although the rock scene has continued to grow and diversify, more recent bands' output has been largely non-polemical, apart from a predilection for extreme volume and abrasive textures. *Éminence grise* Cui Jian continues to enjoy an active career in music and film (even becoming the toast of Cannes) and is revered by those who experienced the heady events of 1989, but his later music has been noncontroversial and anticlimactic; he is increasingly viewed as irrelevant by younger Chinese (if they know of him at all), and no noteworthy figure has arisen to assume his place as the face of defiance. Indeed, one can now find Chinese rock bands that take a hardcore *pro*-government stance, as exemplified in a performance video that went viral during the 2008 Beijing Olympics, in which the local punk band Ordnance bellows at a mixed Chinese and foreign audience, amid a welter of coruscating distortion, "The Olympics have brought a lot of people here from outside the country. We should tell them, Taiwan is OURS!!! Tibet is OURS!!!" Overheated nationalism rules the day.

It is perhaps unsurprising that rock music, the epitome of the individualistic West, never really took root in Chinese soil, given the many ways in which it conflicts with traditional Chinese cultural values. With its preoccupation with personal relationships and self-gratification, rock music cuts against the grain of a society that historically has been more collectivist than individualist in its orientation. In the end, the dream of a Chinese rock-and-roll revolution may well prove to be a snipe hunt, at least until the authoritarian and deeply tradition-bound PRC undergoes an improbable political metamorphosis and grows disillusioned with the comforts of materialism. While it is unwise to count out Chinese rock as a potential force for societal change, it is equally unwise for outside observers with a reformist agenda to expect too much from what is in the end a borrowed musical style. If music is ever to effect broad-based change in China, it will no doubt take the form of a truly indigenous music of resistance.

Of course all these developments were impossible to foresee those many years ago when I first began what would become *Live at the Forbidden City*. At the time, I felt duty-bound to chronicle not only my own absurd personal hijinks, but also what appeared to be the genesis of a truly revolutionary cultural movement. While time and events have tempered my views, I've come to see *Live at the Forbidden City* as an ever more valuable snapshot of a fleeting period of uncommon promise and creativity in China's long, convulsive history. I'm delighted and honored to share the memories with a new generation of readers.

# ACKNOWLEDGEMENTS

*Live at the Forbidden City*—observant readers will note that the title is meant in the metaphorical rather than literal sense—first began to take shape in 1992, when Frank Kouwenhoven of the European Foundation for Chinese Music Research encouraged me to write an account of my musical experiences in Asia for publication in the foundation's journal, *CHIME*. Over the years I gradually expanded my initial narrative to include later events and provide more cultural, historical, and geographical context for the non-specialist reader. I'm exceedingly grateful to Frank for setting this project in motion and for publishing several early excerpts in his organization's indispensable journal.

Of the numerous people who had a hand in making this book a reality, two in particular had especially pivotal roles. First and foremost is my beloved wife, Anne Joiner, who enticed me to China in the first place and without whom none of the experiences described herein would ever have happened. I'm profoundly thankful for Anne's unfailing support of my musical endeavors.

I'm also deeply obliged to my former manager Tang Lei for her invaluable assistance in organizing many of my performances in China, and for helping me to navigate the treacherous shoals of intercultural communication.

For crucial support in the preparation of this manuscript, I'm greatly indebted to my editor, Lisa Costantino, and to Rob Efird, Peter Shotwell, and Larry Trivieri Jr., whose acute editorial perspective and subject matter expertise improved the book immeasurably. In addition, my heartfelt thanks go to Spike Mafford for allowing me to grace the book with his splendid photographs of the Vagaries' 1991 China tour, to Jason Kopec for his striking cover design, and to Jennifer Haywood for her adroit layout skills. Above all, I'm eternally grateful to my publisher at Blue Ear Books, Ethan Casey, for his belief in my work and his stalwart friendship.

For their assistance with my various Asian concert appearances and my research for this book, I'd like to acknowledge the generosity of the Arts International Fund for U.S. Artists Abroad, the Chengdu Guitar Association, Chengdu TV, Chengdu University of Science and Technology, Colin Cowles and the China Institute in New York, Pedro Costa and Maria João of the Instituto Português do Macau, Crystal Records (Taipei), Daniel the videographer, Dirty Roger, Dong Hong, Lisa Dutton, Feng Xiao Cong, John Gilbreath and Seattle's Earshot Jazz organization, the Golden Peacock Hotel (Kunming), Udo Hoffmann and Robert van Kan of the Beijing International Jazz Festival, Victor Huey, Jiang Zhicheng, Andrew Jones, Henry Kwok and Li Chin Sung of Hong Kong's Sound Factory and Noise Asia labels, Lao Zai, Ms. Li at Sichuan Music Conservatory, Liang Weiping, the Macau Jazz Club, the MIDI Music School (Beijing), Trudy Morse and the Malcolm Morse Foundation, Muzak, Inc., New Phase Art Space (Tainan), Mr. Ou and Jazz Music Store (Tainan), the Renmin Hotel (Chongqing), Sichuan Radio, Sichuan TV, Southwest China Fine Arts Institute, Mr. and Mrs. Richard Stites and the U.S. consulate in Guangzhou, Su Li Hua, the Washington State China Relations Council, Woody Wilton, Xiao Fei, Xiao Wei, Xie Gang, Yang Bing, and Yang Shichun of China Record Company's Chengdu branch.

And of course, a hearty *ganbei* to all the musicians who made playing in China and Taiwan such a memorable and life-affirming experience: Roland Barker, Han Bennink, Ryan Berg, Chen Ping, Paul Chénard, Chu Fei, Matthew Clark, Cobra, Alex Crane, Cui Jian, Bruce Culver, Lesli Dalaba, Nicole Darcy, Mike Davidson,

Mark DeForge, Charles Estus, Fréderic Eymard, Tom Fris, Greg Gilmore, Gong Ming, Jeff Greinke, Hua Bin, Huang Qiang, Olli Klomp, Liang Heping, Liu Yuan, Jimmy Luo Ren De, Dave Matthews, Bill Moyer, Shawn "Skip" Nagel, Dominic Rablah, Eddie Randriama Pionona, Bill Rieflin, Charley Rowan, Zhong "Sar" Yongguang, Karl Scheer, Axel Schunn, George Soler, Tao Tao, Guy Taylor, Dave Treanor, "Spike" Tsao Hsin, Andreas Vath, Tom Vest, Wang Xing He, Wang Yong, Bryce Whitwam, Volker Wiedersheim, Yang Chenggang, Zhang Xing, Zhao Xiong, Zhou Di, Zhou Yi, and Zhu Ling.

# Tour Dates

## Dennis Rea Concerts in Sichuan, 1989-90

| Date | City | Venue |
| --- | --- | --- |
| 4/?/1989 | Chengdu | Chengdu University of Science & Technology ("Guitar Party") |
| 4/? | Chengdu | Chengdu University of Science & Technology ("Art Party") |
| 4/4 | Chengdu | Textile Factory #7448 (Chengdu Guitar Association concert) |
| 5/? | Chengdu | Unknown ("Guitar Party" organized by guitar/pipa teacher Feng Ru Jue) |
| 6/3 | Chengdu | Sichuan Conservatory of Music (jazz lecture/concert) |
| ? | Chengdu | Chengdu University of Science & Technology (guitar lecture/concert) |
| ? | Chengdu | Dongfeng Lu Disco |
| ? | Chengdu | Ying Xing Restaurant |
| 11/8 | Chengdu | Liu Xiao Bar |
| 11/16 | Chengdu | Liu Xiao Bar |
| 11/17 | Chengdu | Unknown ("Art Party") |
| 11/26 | Chengdu | Chengdu Workers' Cultural Palace (w/ Zhao Xiong, Zhou Yi) |
| 11/27 | Chengdu | Trade Workers' Hotel Disco |
| 12/20-21 | Chengdu | Chengdu North Sports Arena (w/ Zhang Xing & Yinhuochong) |
| 12/22 | Chengdu | Chengdu University of Science & Technology (two shows, w/ Yinhuochong, Yang Chenggang, Zhao Xiong, Zhou Yi, Wang Xing He) |
| 12/30 | Chengdu | Sichuan-Canada Economic Institute |
| 12/31 | Chengdu | Tianya Dance Hall (w/ Hei Ma) |
| 1/13-15/1990 | Chongqing | Chongqing Sports Arena (w/ Zhang Xing & Yinhuochong, An Dong) |
| 1/15 | Chongqing | Shangri-La Disco |
| 1/16 | Chongqing | Chongqing Sports Arena (w/ Zhang Xing & Yinhuochong, An Dong) |
| 1/17 | Chongqing | Southwest China Art Academy |
| 1/19 | Chengdu | Sichuan Radio Chinese New Year concert (w/ Zhu Ling) |
| 3/10 | Chengdu | Chengdu TV ("Gitar [sic] Music of Dennis Rea"TV special) |
| 3/? | Chengdu | Blue Bar (w/ Yang Chenggang) |

# Identity Crisis 1991 China Tour

| Date | City | Venue |
|------|------|-------|
| 4/6/1991 | Beijing | Maxim's |
| 4/10 | Beijing | Taiwan Hotel (w/Yinhuochong) |
| 4/11 | Beijing | Citli All-Night Club |
| 4/14 | Beijing | Movie House of Panoramic Cinema (a.k.a. Titanium Club) |
| 4/17 | Chengdu | Flying Eagle Beer House |
| 4/19 | Chengdu | Liu Xiao Bar |
| 4/20 | Chengdu | Chengdu University of Science & Technology (two shows) |
| 4/21 | Chengdu | Western Medical University (two shows) |
| 4/22 | Chengdu | Shangri-La "Sing and Dance Hell" (Chengdu TV broadcast) |
| 4/25 | Chengdu | Chengdu Electrical University |
| 4/27 | Guangzhou | Poton 100 |

# The Vagaries 1991 China Tour

| Date | City | Venue |
|------|------|-------|
| 9/21-22/ 1991 | Beijing | Sichuan Provincial Arena (Sichuan-China International TV Festival) |
| 9/24-26 | Beijing | Sichuan Provincial Arena (province-wide TV broadcast) |
| 9/26 | Beijing | Jinhe Hotel Dance Hall (w/ Hei Ma) |
| 9/28-29 | Beijing | Minshan Hotel Dance Hall |
| 9/29 | Chengdu | Night Salon Discothèque |
| 9/30 | Chengdu | Minshan Hotel Dance Hall |
| 10/3 | Chengdu | Chicago Night Club |
| 10/5 | Chengdu | Renmin Hotel |
| 10/5-6 | Chengdu | Chicago Night Club |
| 10/6 | Chengdu | Renmin Hotel |
| 10/8 | Kunming | Yunnan Song & Dance Troupe |
| 10/12 | Kunming | Golden Peacock Hotel |
| 10/13 | Kunming | National Defense Arena |
| 10/19, 22 | Guangzhou | Poton 100 |

# Land 1996 Tour of China, Hong Kong & Macau

| Date | City | Venue |
|---|---|---|
| 11/10/1996 | Beijing | 21st Century Theater (Beijing International Jazz Festival) |
| 11/12 | Beijing | Sunflower Club (w/ Cui Jian, Liang Heping, Liu Xiaosong, Liu Yuan, George Lewis, Steffen Schorn, Claudio Puntin, Andreas Vath) |
| 11/14 | Beijing | Keep in Touch (Wang Yong, Dennis Rea, Lesli Dalaba, Han Bennink, Steffen Schorn, Claudio Puntin) |
| 11/15 | Beijing | Keep in Touch (Wang Yong, George Soler, Bill Moyer, Django Bates, and others) |
| 11/21 | Hong Kong | Fringe Club (w/ Wang Yong) |
| 11/22 | Macau | Largo do Senado (public square) |
| 11/23 | Macau | Jazz Club |
| 11/25-26 | Kunming | Boss Pub |
| 11/29 | Chengdu | Rhinoceros Garden |
| 12/1-2 | Chengdu | New Orleans Jazz Pub (Land spin-off group Nada) |

# BIBLIOGRAPHY

Barmé, Geremie, and John Minford. *Seeds of Fire: Chinese Voices of Conscience*. New York: Hill and Wang, 1988.

Charlton, Hannah, and Jeremy Marre. *Beats of the Heart: Popular Music of the World*. London: Pluto Press, 1985.

Chin, Ava. "China Groove," *The Village Voice*, 12 September 1995.

Cho, Gene Jinsiong. *Lu-Lu: A Study of Its Historical, Acoustical, and Symbolic Significance*. Taipei, Caves Books, Ltd., 1989.

Chong, Woei Lien. "Rock Star Cui Jian: Young China's Voice of the 1980s," *CHIME Journal* 4 (1991).

Choy, Linda. "Musical Heavyweights to Tackle Local Market," *South China Morning Post*, n.d. Couture, Steven. "Rebel Troubadors," *Taipei City Paper*, 14 September 1991.

Cowles, Colin B. "You Can't Always Get What You Want: Rock and Roll, New Cinema, and the Rise of the Individual in Post-Reform China." Ph.D. thesis, n.d.

Devine, Trudy. "Cobra: My Own Private Paradise," *Beijing Scene*, March 1995.

Efird, Robert. "Rock in a Hard Place: Music and the Market in Nineties Beijing," *China Urban: Ethnographies of Contemporary Culture*. Nancy N. Chen and Constance D. Clark, eds. Durham: Duke University Press, 2001.

Everett, Yayoi Uno, and Frederick Lau, eds. *Locating East Asia in Western Art Music*. Middletown: Wesleyan University Press, 2004.

Friedman, Jonathan, ed. *The Routledge History of Social Protest in Popular Music*. New York: Routledge, 2013.

Han, Kuo-huang, and Lindy Li Mark. "Evolution and Revolution in Chinese Music," *Musics of Many Cultures*. Mantle Hood, ed. Berkeley: University of California Press, 1980.

Huang, Cary. "Western Rock Rolls on despite Dissident Tag," *South China Morning Post*, n.d. Jaivin, Linda. "Beijing Bastards: The New Revolution," *CHIME Journal* 8 (1995).

————. "Hou Dejian and the Rise of Pop Music in Taiwan in the Seventies," *CHIME Journal* 9 (1996).

Jones, Andrew F. *Like a Knife: Ideology and Genre in Contemporary Chinese Music*. Ithaca: Cornell University Press, 1992.

————. "Poachers," *Spin*, 1995.

————. *Yellow Music: Media Culture and Colonial Modernity in the Chinese Jazz Age*.

Durham: Duke University Press, 2001.

Kraus, Richard Curt. *Pianos and Politics in China*. New York: Oxford University Press, 1989. Kuo, Kaiser. "The New Long Mosh," *Time Asia*, 2 September 2002.

Lai, T. C., and Robert Mok. *Jade Flute: The Story of Chinese Music*. New York: Schocken Books, 1981.

Law, S. L. "Cui Belts Out a Message but Doesn't Rock the Boat," *South China Morning Post*, n.d.

Lii, Jane H. "And Now, Direct from Tiananmen Square, a New Star," *New York Times*, 28 August 1995.

Lim, Louisa. *The People's Republic of Amnesia: Tiananmen Revisited*. New York: Oxford University Press, 4 June 2014.

Liu, Joyce. "Son of Betel-Nut Vendor Rocks in Taiwanese," Reuter Taipei Bureau, n.d.

Malm, William P. *Music Cultures of the Pacific, the Near East, and Asia*. New Jersey: Prentice-Hall, Englewood Cliffs, 1967.

Manuel, Peter. *Popular Musics of the Non-Western World*. New York: Oxford University Press, 1988.

Martens, Bill. "All That Jazz," *Asia Times*, November 1996.

Micic, Peter. "Notes on Pop/Rock Genres in the Eighties in China," *CHIME Journal* 8 (1995). Miller, Jeffrey. "Taiwan's Crystal Sounds," *Taipei City Paper*, 14 September 1991.

Mingyue, Liang. *Music of the Billion*. New York: Heinrichshofen Edition, 1985. Moser, David. "The Book of Changes: Jazz in Beijing," *Jazz Now* 6, no. 1 (1996). Myers, John E. *The Way of the Pipa*. Ohio: Kent State University Press, 1992.

Nip, Alan. "Voice of Protest Defies Officialdom," *South China Morning Post*, n.d.

Pareles, Jon. "Chinese Rock Legend Sings of a Different Malaise," *New York Times*, 28 August 1995.

———. "New Wave Styles Return on a Visit from Beijing," *New York Times*, 31 August 1996. Perkins, Christl, and Steven Schwankert. "All That Jazz," *Beijing Scene* 2, no. 25 (1996).

Peters, Matt. "Rock 'N' Revolt," *Far Eastern Economic Review*, 28 March 1991.

Rea, Dennis. "A Western Musician's View of China's Rock and Pop Scene," *CHIME Journal* 6 (1993).

Rea, Dennis. "Cui Jian Makes U.S. Debut in Seattle," *CHIME Journal* 8 (1995).

Rea, Dennis. "The LAND Tour and the Rise of Jazz in China," *CHIME Journal* 10 (1999).

Rea, Dennis. "Ambushed from All Sides: Rock Music as a Force for Change in China," *Routledge History of Social Protest in Popular Music*. New York: Routledge (2013).

Qianhong, Fu. "New Breed of Jazz Hits China," *China Daily* 4, no. 179 (13 November 1996).

Rees, Helen. *Echoes of History: Naxi Music in Modern China*. New York: Oxford University Press, 2000.

Rose, Jon. "Our Man in Hong Kong," *Coda Magazine* 274 (July/August 1997). Schell, Orville. *Mandate of Heaven*. New York: Simon & Schuster, 1994. Schwankert, Steven. "Rock in Opposition," *The Wire* No. 139 (1995).

Southerland, Daniel. "Pop Star's 'Long March' Is Cut Short," Washington Post Service, n.d. Spence, Jonathan D. The Search for Modern China. New York: W.W. Norton & Company, 1990.

Stevens, K. Mark, and Wehrfritz, George E. Southwest China Off the Beaten Track. Lincolnwood, IL: Passport Books, 1988.

Tanenbaum, David. "Bad Day in the People's Republic," *Guitar Player* (March 1989). Tyler, Patrick E. "For the Rockers Now, China Is a Very Hard Place," New York Times, 9 January 1995.

Tyson, James L. "Making Music, Making Waves," *The Christian Science Monitor*, 11 September 1991.

Wester, Michael. "PRC Invades Taiwan with Rock Music," *The China News* 1, no. 60 (1994). Wiant, Bliss. *The Music of China*, Chung Chi Publications, Hong Kong, 1965.

Yule, Qian. "Jazzing It Up," *China Daily* 4, no. 179 (13 November 1996).

————. "One Man's Mission to Fill the World with Jazz," *China Daily* 4, no. 179 (13 November 1996).

# DISCOGRAPHY

*Note that many of the titles in this discography are out of print, difficult to find, or available only in China.*

ADO. *ADO*. China Tourism Audio Video Publishing BJZ 01, 1989. Chen Yi. *Duo Ye*. China Records AL-57, 1986.

Cui Jian. *The Power of the Powerless*. Released in the USA by World Beat Records, 1999 <http://www.wbeat.com>.

Cui Jian. *1986–1996*. Jingwen Records, 1996. Cui Jian. *Balls under the Red Flag*. 1994.

Cui Jian. *Rock and Roll on the New Long March*. China Tourism Audio Video Publishing TAV9-5, 1991.

Cui Jian. *Solution*. UFO Records UFO-91172, 1991. Dadawa. *Sister Drum*. UFO/Sire 61889-2, 1995.

Dancing Stone. *Normal Free*. Sound Factory SFCD 006, 1993.

Dayan Ancient Music Association. *Naxi Music From Lijiang*. Nimbus Records NI 5510 1997. The Fly. *The Fly*. Hardcore Pop Company, 1999.

Gao Ping. *Jazz in China*. China Record Company FL-128, 1988.

Guo Wenjing, *Shu Dao Nan*. Chongqing Huaxia Record & Video Co. HXS 8709, 1987.

He Yong. *Garbage Dump*. Rock Records/Magic Stone Y-1132, 1994.

Hiu, Nelson. *Music for Roaches, Birds, and Other Creatures*. Sound Factory SFCD 014, 1995.

*Instrumental Music of the Uighurs*. King Record Co. KICC 5138, 1991. Jazz Cowboys. *Jazz Cowboys*. Crystal Records CIRD 1011-2, 1991.

Lao Ge. Crystal Records CIRD 1025-2, 1994. Li Chin Sung. *Past*. Tzadik TZ 7014, 1996.

Liu Sola. *Blues in the East*. Axiom 314-524 003-2, 1994.

Lo Ka Ping. *Lost Sounds of the Tao*. World Arbiter 2004, 2001.

*Music of the Yi People in Yunnan, China,* vols. 1 and 2. King Record Co. KICC 5188 and 5213, 1995, 1996.

Qu Xiaosong. *Mong Dong.* China Records AL-55, 1986.

Rea, Dennis. *Shadow in Dreams.* Sichuan China Records FL-176, 1990.

Sheng Xiang & Water3. *Getting Dark.* Trees Music & Art TMCD-330, 2004. Sola and Wu Man. *China Collage.* Avant AVAN 046, 1996.

Sun Guoqing, Li Lingyu, a.o. *The Red Sun.* China Record Corporation (Shanghai) SCD-9201, 1992.

Tan Dun, *Nine Songs: Ritual Opera.* CRI 603, 1990. Tan Dun. *Shan Yao.* China Records AL-42, 1986.

Tang Dynasty. *Tang Dynasty.* Rock Records/Magic Stone RC-303, 1992.

Various artists. *Beijing Band 2001: New Rock Bands from the People's Republic of China.* Kemaxiu Music, 2003.

Various artists. *China Fire I.* Rock Records/Magic Stone RC-349, 1992. Various artists. *China Fire II.* Rock Records/Magic Stone MSC-020, 1996.

Various artists (Dou Wei, Zhang Chu, He Yong, Tang Dynasty). *Live in Hong Kong.* Rock Records/Magic Stone MSD-002, 1994.

Various artists. *No. 43 Baojia Street.* Youdai Productions, 1996.

Various artists. *Peking Punks: Beloved Party.* Sickboy Productions, 1997.

Various artists. *Shanghai Jazz: Musical Seductions from China's Age of Decadence.* EMI 489 701021 001 9, 2003.

Various artists. *Shanghai Lounge Divas.* EMI 7243 4 73058 25, 2004. Various artists. *Tellus #19: New Music China,* n.d.

Various artists. *What's Sound,* vol. 2. Sound Factory SFCD 007, 1993. Wang Lei. *Spring Is Here.* Autobahn ATB001, 1998.

Wang Yong. *Samsara.* Rock Records/Magic Stone MSD-007, 1996.

Wang Yong/Han Bennink/Dennis Rea/Andreas Schreiber/Claudio Puntin/Steffen Schorn/Lesli Dalaba. *Free Touching: Live in Beijing at Keep in Touch.* Noise Asia NAKIT 01/02 CD, n.d.

Wu Bai. *China Blue*. Rock Records RC-450, 1994.

Xinjiang Song and Dance Troupe. *Music of Xinjiang*. BMG Hong Kong 74321 18460-2, 1993.

Ye Xiaogang. *Horizon*. China Records AL-51, 1986.

Zhang Xing. *Zai Hui Dao(?)*. Shenzhen Records AC-2096.

Zhou Long. *Guang Ling San*. China Records AL-52, 1986.

# About the Author

*Photo by Daniel Sheehan*

Dennis Rea's adventurous guitar playing blends modern jazz, creative rock, experimental music, and world musical traditions into his own unique approach, marked by haunting lyricism, enigmatic textures, agile improvisation, and the raw dynamism of rock.

Over the years Dennis has led or been a key contributor to such innovative groups as LAND, Iron Kim Style, Stackpole, Savant, and Earthstar, and is perhaps best known for his work with internationally acclaimed MoonJune Records artists Moraine. He has performed or recorded with numerous prominent creative musicians including acclaimed French composer Hector Zazou, Dutch jazz legend Han Bennink, trombone virtuoso Stuart Dempster, and godfather of Chinese rock Cui Jian, as well as members of King Crimson, Hawkwind, R.E.M., Pearl Jam, Soundgarden, Ministry, and the Sun Ra Arkestra. He has performed on three continents at prestigious venues and festivals such as NEARfest, WOMAD, Beijing International Jazz Festival, Sichuan-China International TV Festival, MuzEnergo Tour (Russia), Baja Prog (Mexico), Bumbershoot Arts Festival, Voice of Nomads Festival (Siberia), Northwest Folklife Festival, and Earshot Jazz Festival. As detailed in this book, he has collaborated with many of the most important figures in contemporary Chinese music and was one of the first Western musicians to record an album for the state-owned China Record Company. His activities have spanned film, theater, radio, and modern dance, and he has appeared on more than three dozen recordings to date.

He has been awarded grants for his musical activities by the U. S. State Department (Fulbright-Hays program), Arts International

Fund for U.S. Artists Abroad, Seattle Arts Commission, King County Arts Commission, Malcolm S. Morse Foundation, and Jack Straw Foundation, and received funding and/or encouragement to conduct research for this book from the Washington State China Relations Council, European Foundation for Chinese Music Research, and New York's China Institute. He has been interviewed by National Public Radio and other nationally syndicated radio programs and by numerous publications, and has acted as a panelist or consultant for the Experience Music Project, Seattle Art Museum, Seattle Asian Art Museum, Seattle Center, and the Urban Institute.

Dennis Rea has also been active as a professional writer and editor for more than 25 years, bringing his wide-ranging musical, cultural, and geographical expertise to bear in his contributions to numerous music and regional news publications. He has written extensively about Chinese music for publications including the *Routledge History of Social Protest in Popular Music*, the *Routledge Encyclopedia of Contemporary Chinese Culture*, and *CHIME: The Journal of the European Foundation for Chinese Music Research*. In the late 1990s he co-published the *Tentacle* journal of Pacific Northwest creative music. As a former co-producer of the Seattle Improvised Music Festival and Other Sounds new-music concert series and a current organizer of the Zero-G Concert Series and Seaprog festival of progressive/art rock, he has presented dozens of the world's finest experimental and improvising musicians to Pacific Northwest audiences.

For more information on Dennis Rea's activities, visit:

www.dennisrea.com
www.liveattheforbiddencity.com

## Dennis Rea Selected Discography

### Dennis Rea
*Black River Transect* (MoonJune Records, 2015)
*Views from Chicheng Precipice* (MoonJune Records, 2010)
*Shadow in Dreams* (China Record Company, 1990)

### With Moraine:
*Groundswell* (MoonJune Records, 2014)
*Metamorphic Rock: Live at NEARfest* (MoonJune Records, 2011)
*Manifest Density* (MoonJune Records, 2009)

### With LAND:
*Road Movies* (First World Music, 2001)
*Archipelago* (Periplum, 1997)
*LAND* (Extreme, 1995)

### With Earthstar:
*Atomkraft? Nein Danke!* (Sky, 1982)
*French Skyline* (Sky, 1981)
*Salterbarty Tales* (Moontower, 1979)

### With others:
With Hector Zazou: *Strong Currents* (Materiali Sonori Sonora Portraits, 2003)

With Han Bennink, Wang Yong, Andreas Schreiber, Steffen Schorn, Claudio Puntin, Lesli Dalaba, a.o.: *Free Touching: Live in Beijing at Keep in Touch* (Noise Asia, 2004)

With Iron Kim Style: *Iron Kim Style* (MoonJune Records, 2010)

With Savant: *The Neo-Realist (At Risk)* (Palace of Lights, 1983/2002)

With Stackpole: *Stackpole* (First World Music, 2001)

With The Shredders: *Shredder Orpheus - Music from the Original Motion Picture Soundtrack* (Light in the Attic Records / Traction.TV Trac-01, 2014)

With Tempered Steel: *Tempered Steel* (Nunatak, 2012)

With the Jim Cutler Jazz Orchestra: *Gimme Some Sugar, Baby!* (Jamco, 2014)